Carl Philipp Emanuel Bach
Johann Friedrich Agricola
Lorenz Christoph Mizler

THE NEKROLOG OR
OBITUARY NOTICE OF
JOHANN SEBASTIAN BACH
TRANSLATED INTO ENGLISH
WITH AN INTRODUCTION
NOTES AND TWO
APPENDICES
BY WALTER EMERY

MCMXLII

Travis & Emery Music Bookshop

THE NEKROLOG OR
OBITUARY NOTICE OF
JOHANN SEBASTIAN BACH
TRANSLATED INTO ENGLISH
WITH AN INTRODUCTION
NOTES AND TWO
APPENDICES
BY WALTER EMERY

Facsimile of 1942 translation.

Published Travis & Emery 2010.

Published by
Travis & Emery Music Bookshop
17 Cecil Court, London, WC2N 4EZ,
United Kingdom.
(+44) 20 7240 2129
neworders@travis-and-emery.com

Hardback: 978-1-906857-79-0
Paperback: 978-1-906857-80-6.

THE NEKROLOG OR
OBITUARY NOTICE OF
JOHANN SEBASTIAN BACH
TRANSLATED INTO ENGLISH
WITH AN INTRODUCTION
NOTES AND TWO
APPENDICES
BY WALTER EMERY

MCMXLII

We are grateful to Professor Yo Tomita, School of Music & Sonic Arts, Queen's University Belfast, for allowing us to include this review in this publication:

This book is a facsimile reproduction of a recently-resurfaced fair copy manuscript of Walter Emery (1909-74), the influential English Bach scholar, active in the mid-20th century. The manuscript is Emery's own English translation of Bach's obituary notice, written jointly by C.P.E. Bach and J.F. Agricola, originally published in Mizler's *Neu Eröffnete Musikalischer Bibliothek*, volume 4, part 1 in Leipzig 1754. Also included are two short biographical excerpts on Bach: J.G. Walther's *Musikalisches Lexicon* (1732) and the Genealogy which Bach himself compiled in c.1735.

From the facsimile it appears that the MS is neatly assembled and comes complete with title-page, dedication, contents page and notes. Dates are given in several places: '1942' on the title-page; the heading of the dedication (p.i): 'To Betty: 29 March 1942' (Emery's first wife); and at the end of the volume (p.231): 'Begun at Bedford in October 1941; continued at Market Warsop, and finished 19 Jan. 1942'.

The MS comes from the period when Emery's musical career was interrupted by the War and he served in the Royal Army. However, the methodical approach with which the MS is put together clearly reflects that Emery was a fully-focused scholar of Bach's organ works. Had it been published immediately, it would have been the first English translation of these primary source references in Bach studies, preceding *The Bach Reader - A Life of Johann Sebastian Bach in Letters and Documents,* edited by Hans T. David and Arthur Mendel (New York: W.W. Norton, 1945).

The appearance of *The Bach Reader* must have come as a shock to Emery. His annoyance is clearly felt in his critical review of the work, published in *The Musical Times*, lxxxvii/1243 (Sept. 1946), pp.268-269. In addition to listing numerous errors (which were all corrected in the revised edition of 1966), Emery concludes on a bitter note: 'owing to its [*Bach Reader*'s] plan and its frequently unidiomatic English, it is less readable than the standard works'. His frustration becomes more understandable if we compare the openings of both translations:

Emery (1942): JOHANN SEBASTIAN BACH belonged to a family whose every member seems to have had, as a natural gift, a fondness for music and ability in its practice. At least it is certain that, from the founder of the family (Veit Bach) to his descendants of the seventh and present generation, all the Bachs have been devoted to music; and further, with one or two possible exceptions, they have all made it their profession.

Bach Reader (1945/1966; New Bach Reader 1998): Johann Sebastian Bach belongs to a family that seems to have received a love and aptitude for music as a gift of Nature to all its members in common. So much is certain, that Veit Bach, the founder of the family, and all his descendants, even to the present seventh generation, have been devoted to music, and all save perhaps a very few have made it their profession.

Unlike the text presented in *The Bach Reader*, Emery not only provides a helpful introduction but also supplements numerous and extensive endnotes, which occupy almost two thirds of the book. There he records not only corrections and additional information which he had sourced in then available literature (mainly from C.S. Terry's *Bach. A Biography* of 1928, the book he considered to represent 'the latest modern research'), but also his own insightful 'guesses' and notes for future research. This is in fact the most valuable part of the manscript. While it is true that some of Emery's information now requires correction (e.g. St John Passion was first performed in 1723 [*recte* 1724]; the Goldberg Variations were published in 1742 [*recte* 1741]), the volume reminds us that some of the old debates should not be forgotten. One of these debates regards the validity of C.P.E.'s claim that Volumier arranged the Dresden contest of Bach and Marchand; Emery wonders if Bach visited Dresden in order to hear Marchand, and the contest was arranged there and then (p.112).

Emery, unfortunately, never found an opportunity to publish his book. In the next two decades, Bach scholarship evolved very rapidly - a fact of which Emery was fully aware, as we learn from the numerous reviews he wrote in the subsequent years. To the 21st-century scholar, the publication of this manuscript, with all its defects, represents a valuable historical record of a young and brilliant scholar who sought to uncover the facts about Bach's life and strove to produce a superior English translation of one of the most important primary sources.

Yo Tomita, Belfast, 12 May 2009

THE NEKROLOG

THE NEKROLOG OR
OBITUARY NOTICE OF
JOHANN SEBASTIAN BACH
TRANSLATED INTO ENGLISH
WITH AN INTRODUCTION
NOTES AND TWO
APPENDICES
BY WALTER EMERY

MCMXLII

CONTENTS

Dedicatory Note	page i
Introduction	xiii
Text of the Nekrolog	1
Appendix I	69
Appendix II	75
Notes	79
Postscript	227

TO BETTY : 29 MARCH 1942

IT MAY ONE DAY be my misfortune to have to deal biographically with Bach, as an introduction to the study of his organ works that I hope in time to find material for. Even if I never rise so high, I must still make myself acquainted with the facts of his life; not that I expect to find therein any confirmation of the vulgar notion that a composer writes a love-song because he has just found a new mistress (for that matter, the old boy

THE NEKROLOG

does not seem to have indulged in such luxuries); but an editor never knows when some odd bit of apparently disconnected information will fall into place and settle a problem.

For my purpose I must not only read up the material that passes for Bach biography in the works of the standard authors; I must know how much of this material is solid fact (i.e., directly drawn from such documents as the registers of churches, courts, and town councils), how much is reasonably likely to be true (e.g., statements of authors up to the time of Forkel, most, if not all,

DEDICATORY NOTE

of whom were acquainted with Bach either themselves or at only one remove), and how much is mere guesswork, provided by later biographers in order to connect or explain the facts at their disposal. (I am not attempting to disparage the work of the standard authors. A vast amount of such guesswork is essential, and much of what has been done must come near the truth.) An obvious step in this necessary inquiry is to read all the early writings on Bach (which, thank the Lord, are not so very numerous), and this I have begun to do.

THE NEKROLOG

The first notice of Bach in a reference book is the article in Walther's LEXICON of 1732, of which I give a translation in Appendix I.

Then there is the bare outline of Bach's life up to c. 1736 given in the Genealogy (Appendix II).

About this time there appeared some casual references to Bach and his works, and Scheibe made his attack on Bach — the beginning of a series of tedious controversial articles which nevertheless contains some important matter. These writings are not at present available to me

DEDICATORY NOTE   v

(I was fool enough not to buy the Scheibe when I had the chance), and to go into them properly will involve work in the British Museum. They are therefore not dealt with here.

Then in 1754, four years after Bach's death, appeared his belated obituary notice, commonly known as the NEKROLOG. The translation of this forms the bulk of the present book.

On each of these texts I have commented either in the Introduction or the Notes. The latter are a very mixed bag. Some are essential corrections. Some contain additional matter that

THE NEKROLOG

I thought might interest you. One or two merely record guesses of my own, which need to be backed up by more evidence before they can be published, but which I don't want to forget. At one time I intended to make the notes very much more comprehensive, and to include among them general discussions of the music and the way in which Bach's style changed as he grew older, came under new influences, and found at his disposal new instrumental and vocal media; but I came to the conclusion that without reference books this would be impossible;

DEDICATORY NOTE

and further, as at present I have little to add to the writings of the standard authors, I should for the most part have been simply re-hashing well-known material. The result would have justified neither the labour involved nor the risk of damaging my not valueless books by keeping them in the conditions I am at present living in.

Most of the translation was done last winter. Mrs Cocker at Novellos helped me with some of the more contorted sentences; but there were some that puzzled her and others that I forgot to ask

THE NEKROLOG

her about. However, the translation (though by no means literal) is as accurate as I can make it; and indeed I think that in the prose the sense of it is right enough: what I have missed here and there is the exact meaning of such phrases as 'auf das Verdienst seines Erlösers ... verschied' — obviously a pious euphemism which it would have been pleasant to translate instead of using the bald 'died'. As for the LIBRETTO at the end, I have had no help with it at all (except that you have given me the dictionary meanings of certain

DEDICATORY NOTE

words), and have had to guess a good deal. Fortunately the thing is of no importance, whether as biography or literature.

The Introduction and Notes are of a rather formal cast because I might one day publish the work more or less as it stands, but with the addition of the other early writings that I cannot deal with at present; and I thought I might as well get the material into shape and be done with it.

Now read the Postscript (p. 227). I am sorry

x   THE NEKROLOG

that I could not finish the job in time for Christmas (my original intention); but anyway, here it is. It has done me good, and I hope you will find this account of the Trials of an Organist not unamusing in parts.

INTRODUCTION

THE SO-CALLED NEKROLOG appeared in the last number issued of Lorenz Christoph Mizler's NEU ERÖFFNETER MUSIKALISCHER BIBLIOTHEK (Bd. iv, Teil i, Leipzig 1754); this was the official organ of the Society of Musical Sciences founded by Mizler. The authors' names are not given; but in a letter to Forkel dated 13 Jan. 1775 Emanuel Bach says, ' The account of my late father's life in Mizler, dearest friend, was put together by the late Agricola and myself in Berlin; Mizler added to it only the portion that begins at the words "He joined the Society" and continues to the end. It is not worth much. The deceased, like myself and all true musicians, was no lover of dry mathematical matters."[x]

Philipp Emanuel Bach, Sebastian's second son, lived at home until 1734. Johann Friedrich Agricola was a pupil of Bach's from

[x] Bach-Urkunden, N.B.G. xvii, 3; 1917.

INTRODUCTION

1738 to 1741. Owing to its authorship, therefore, and despite its occasional errors, the Nekrolog is a historical document of some importance. It was the first attempt at a full-length biography of Bach and a critical appreciation of his work as composer and performer (the notice in Walther's LEXICON of 1732 being necessarily incomplete); and directly or indirectly it has been used by all subsequent biographers.

The earlier parts of the MUSIKALISCHER BIBLIOTHEK are not uncommon books;

but Band iv Teil i, a small book and easily lost, has become something of a rarity. (I have been unable to trace a copy in England.) Despite this fact and the importance of the Nekrolog, the full text of the latter was never reprinted until 1920[x], when B.F. Richter edited it for the Bach-Jahrbuch. The present is the first English translation: a free version based on Richter's text, but including the Canon, which he omitted. I regret that my ability

[x] The LIBRETTO appeared in Bitter's biography, 1st edition, 1865.

INTRODUCTION xvii

as a versifier does not enable me to do justice to Dr Georg Wenzky's LIBRETTO.

As Appendices I give translations of the article on Bach in Johann Gottfried Walther's MUSIKALISCHES LEXICON (1732), and the entry concerning him in the Genealogy (the wording probably Sebastian's own, and the date of the entry c. 1736).

Square brackets indicate editorial additions and alterations. The small superimposed figures refer to the Notes at the end of the book. I have altered old-fashioned spellings of place- and personal names to agree with those now in common use, and have taken some 'typographical' liberties.

It looks as if the biographical portions of the Nekrolog (exasperatingly meagre, considering the unrivalled advantages enjoyed by its authors) were based on the Genealogy; Emanuel had a copy of this, and both texts give an incorrect date for Bach's appointment to Arnstadt. Musically, Emanuel and Agricola were more concerned with the excellence of Bach's organ- and clavier-playing than with

INTRODUCTION　　　　　　　　xix

that of his compositions. To-day our attitude is very much the reverse. Fortunately the purely musical critics, unlike the pure biographers and the miserable textual critics, have plenty of material to work on — the forty-odd fat volumes of the B.G.; and there is no need to expatiate here on the well-known characteristics of Bach's works, or on their musical value.

In compiling the Notes I was chiefly concerned to correct and comment on the Nekrolog's errors; but I have provided some extra information, so that the book as a whole may serve as a short biography, of peculiar interest owing to its origin, from which the interested reader may pass on to the more elaborate studies for which we have to thank the labours of more modern authors.

THE TEXT OF THE NEKROLOG

[MIZLER records the deaths of Georg Heinrich Bümler and Gottfried Heinrich Stölzel, and continues:]

THE THIRD AND LAST IS THE HIGH-BORN HERR JOHANN SEBASTIAN BACH, WORLD-RENOWNED AS AN ORGANIST, COURT COMPOSER TO THE KING OF POLAND AND ELECTOR OF SAXONY, AND DIRECTOR OF MUSIC IN LEIPZIG.

JOHANN SEBASTIAN BACH belonged to a family whose every member seems to have had, as a natural gift, a fondness for music and ability in its practice. At least it is certain that, from the founder of the family (Veit Bach) to his descendants of the seventh and present generation, all the Bachs have been devoted to music; and further, with one or two possible exceptions, they have all made it their profession![1] This Veit was exiled from Hungary in the sixteenth century, for religious reasons; he later settled in Thuringia, in which province a number of his descendants also have made their homes.[2]

SOME EARLY BACHS

Among the many members of the Bach family that have distinguished themselves in the practice of music, or the construction of new musical instruments, the following (besides our Johann Sebastian) are particularly remarkable as having been composers:

1 Heinrich Bach [b.1615], organist at Arnstadt, who died in 1692

2 and 3 his two sons: Johann Christoph [b.1642], Court and Town Organist at Eisenach, who died in 1703: and Johann Michael [1648-94], organist and parish

clerk in the Gehren district, who was Johann Sebastian's first father-in-law

4 Johann Ludwig Bach [1677-1741], Ducal Capellmeister at Meiningen

5 Johann Bernhard Bach [b. 1676], chamber-musician and organist at Eisenach, who passed away in 1749.

Ample evidence of all these men's ability as composers, both in vocal and instrumental forms, is provided by their extant works. The above-mentioned Johann Christoph, especially, had a gift for the invention of

JOHANN CHRISTOPH BACH

beautiful themes, as well as for setting words expressively. He composed (so far, that is, as the taste of his day would permit) both in the galant or singing style and in extra-ordinarily full polyphony. The first statement is borne out by a motet of his, composed more than seventy years ago; at which early date, apart from other striking touches, he was bold enough to use the chord of the augmented sixth. As for the second statement, he composed a Church Cantata in twenty-two obbligato parts, whose harmony is nevertheless flawlessly pure throughout; and it is equally noteworthy that on the organ and clavier he never played in less than five real parts.[3]

Johann Bernhard composed a number of fine overtures in the Telemann style.

It would seem strange that men so worthy should have remained so little known outside their own province, did we not remember that these honest Thuringians were so content with their fatherland and their circumstances that never once would they venture upon following

THE EARLY BACHS

their fortune far away. The applause of the
noblemen in whose domains they were born,
and that of a host of their simple-hearted
fellow-countrymen, was theirs already; and
this they greatly preferred to the encomiums,
to be won (if at all) only with difficulty and
expense, of strangers fewer in number and
most probably envious. It is, meanwhile,
our duty to refresh and keep green the memory
of worthy men; and this will amply justify
us before those who may, perhaps, think this
little digression upon the musical history of

THE NEKROLOG

the Bach family too long and detailed. We return to our Johann Sebastian.[4]

HE WAS BORN AT EISENACH on 21 Mar. 1685.[5] His parents were Johann Ambrosius Bach, Court and Town Musician there, and Elisabeth (née Lämmerhirt), whose father was an alderman at Erfurt.[6] Sebastian's father had a twin brother named Johann Christoph,[7] who was a Court and Town Musician at Arnstadt. These two brothers were so alike in everything — even to the state of

BACH AT OHRDRUF

their health and their musical ability — that when they were together they could be told apart only by their clothes.

Johann Sebastian found himself orphaned before he was ten years old. He moved to Ohrdruf, and was taken in by his eldest brother Johann Christoph[8], who was organist there; under the latter's guidance he laid the foundations of his clavier technique. Our little Johann Sebastian was, even at that tender age, extraordinarily eager to extend his knowledge of music. In a very short time he mastered all the pieces that his brother was willing to give him for his instruction; but his brother had also a book full of clavier works by the then celebrated masters Froberger, Kerl, and Pachelbel; and this, despite all his entreaties, was forbidden to him. Who knows why? In his eagerness to make further progress he thought of the following innocent trick: The book was kept in a cupboard, which had only a latticed door. With his small hands he was able to reach through the lattice, and, as the book was bound

OHRDRUF: THE MS. BOOK

in paper only, to roll it up and withdraw it. This he did at night, when all were in bed; and as he was never able to strike a light, he copied the book by moonlight. After six months this musical prize was safely in his hands, and with the greatest eagerness he attempted to make use of it in secret; but, to his intense distress, his brother found him out and unmercifully deprived him of his copy, made with such great labour. To appreciate our little Johann Sebastian's grief over this loss, we have only to think of a miser that has lost a ship on the way to Peru with a hundred thousand thalers. He did not regain the book until after his brother's death.⁹ And is it not possible that this very anxiety to make progress in music, and the labour expended upon the book in question, were incidentally responsible for his death? as we shall see later.

After his brother died
[In the year 1700] Johann Sebastian betook himself to St. Michael's Gymnasium at Lüneburg, in company with a schoolfellow of his named Erdmann; who died, not

BACH AT LÜNEBURG

very many years ago, at Danzig, as a Baron and Resident of the Tsar of Russia's."[10]

Our Bach was well received at Lüneburg, on account of his unusually fine soprano voice. Some time afterwards, in the choir one day, he found himself singing, besides the soprano notes that he was supposed to produce, those an octave lower at the same time; and this unconsciously, and indeed against his will. His voice behaved in this quite new way for eight days, during which time he could neither speak nor sing but in octaves. After that he lost the soprano notes, and therewith his fine voice.

From Lüneburg he sometimes made his way to Hamburg, to hear the then celebrated organist of St. Catherine's Church, Johann Adam Reinken. Here also he had the opportunity of becoming thoroughly familiar with the French style, which at that time and in that neighbourhood was quite new, by frequent listening to a band, then famous, maintained by the Duke of Celle and consisting for the most part of Frenchmen."

WEIMAR & ARNSTADT

In 1703 he came to Weimar[12], and became a Court Musician there. Later in the same year he was appointed organist of the New Church at Arnstadt[13]. Here he displayed the real first-fruits of his diligent study of the arts of organ-playing and composition; which latter he had learnt, for the most part, only from examining the works of composers then famous and regarded as profound, and putting into practice the results of his study. In his organ compositions he took as models the works of Bruhns, Reinken, Buxtehude,

and certain good French organists[14]. He was
particularly desirous of hearing good
organists as much as he possibly could;
and here at Arnstadt this desire moved him
to set out for Lübeck[15] — what is more, on
foot — to hear Dietrich Buxtehude, the
famous organist of St. Mary's Church in
that city. He stayed at Lübeck, not without
profit, for nearly three months; not until then
did he turn back to Arnstadt.

In 1707 he was appointed organist of the
church of St. Blasius, Mühlhausen[16]. This

WEIMAR

town, however, was not to have the satisfaction of keeping him long; for in the following year a visit to Weimar brought with it an opportunity of playing before the Duke; the result was that he was offered a position as chamber [musician] and Court Organist: an offer that he immediately accepted.[7] His gracious master's delight in his playing encouraged him to exert himself to the utmost to master the art of managing the organ; and it was here that he composed most of his organ works.[18] In 1714 he was made Concertmeister at the same Court; but as such his duties at that time consisted chiefly in composing and performing Church Cantatas'.⁹ At Weimar he trained not a few competent organists; among whom Johann Caspar Vogler, his second successor at Weimar itself, is most deserving of mention.

After the death of Zachau, Director of Music and Organist at the Market Church in Halle, our Bach received an invitation to that post. He did in fact visit Halle, and performed a test-piece there; but he found

MARCHAND AT DRESDEN

good reasons for refusing the post, which was afterwards obtained by Kirchhof.[20]

In 1717 our Bach, already so famous, had a further opportunity of adding to his renown. Marchand, celebrated in France as a clavier-player and organist, had come to Dresden and played before the King to the latter's particular satisfaction; and had been so fortunate as to be offered a position at Court with a generous salary. Volumier, who was then Concertmeister at Dresden, was not unacquainted with Bach's merits; and wrote to him at

Weimar, inviting him to come to Dresden without delay and challenge the arrogant Marchand to a musical contest for the preëminence. Bach readily accepted this invitation, and set out for Dresden. Volumier received him with open arms, and arranged for him to hear his opponent beforehand, in secret. After this Bach invited Marchand to the contest in a courteous private letter, wherein he professed his readiness to perform extempore any musical task that Marchand should set him, if Marchand would do the same in return.

BACH AND MARCHAND

Great audacity, to be sure! Marchand readily accepted the challenge. Time and place were settled, not without the King's knowledge; and at the appointed time Bach was to be found on the field of battle, in the house of a certain eminent minister, where there was gathered a great company of persons, of high rank and of both sexes. They waited long for Marchand. Finally, the owner of the house sent to Marchand's lodgings to remind him, in case he should have forgotten, that now was the time to show himself a man. But, to their great surprise, they found that early in the morning of that same day Monsieur Marchand had left Dresden by special post. Bach, thus left sole master of the field, had in consequence opportunity enough of demonstrating the strength with which he was armed against his opponent; and this he did, to the wonder of all those present. As a reward, the King set aside for him a present of 500 thalers; but of this he was deprived through the dishonesty of a certain official, who thought he could make a better use of this present; and

BACH AND MARCHAND

had to return home with the honour he had acquired as the sole return for his labours. A strange fatality! A Frenchman voluntarily forsakes the substantial salary (of more than a thousand thalers) that was offered him; and the German whom, as is obvious from his flight, he regarded as his superior, cannot obtain so much as part of the single present destined for him by the King's bounty! For the rest, our Bach freely admitted that Marchand was a neat and fine executant; but whether Marchand's *Musettes for Christmas Night*, whose composition and performance had won him the greatest fame in Paris, would before connoisseurs have been able to hold their own against the manifold variety of Bach's fugues, let them decide who heard them both in their strength."[21]

After our Bach's return to Weimar, and still in the same year, he was appointed Capellmeister to Leopold, at that time Prince of Anhalt-Cöthen, and a great connoisseur and lover of music.[22] He entered upon his duties immediately, and discharged them,

BACH AT HAMBURG

to the very great satisfaction of his gracious prince, for nearly six years. During this time, in about the year 1722[23], he visited Hamburg; and there played, to the general wonderment, for more than two hours upon the fine organ of St. Catharine's Church, before the magistracy and many other notables of the town. The old organist of this church, Johann Adam Reinken (who at that time was nearly a hundred years of age), listened to him with particular satisfaction, and paid him the following compliment, 'I thought this art was dead; but I see that it yet lives in you' — referring especially to the chorale 'An Wasserflüssen Babylon', upon which our Bach had, at the request of those present, extemporized at great length (for nearly half an hour) and in various styles, just as in former days the best of the Hamburg organists had been accustomed to do at ~~Sunday~~ Saturday Vespers. Such appreciation was the less to be expected of Reinken because, many years before, he had worked out this very chorale in the very same style; which,

LEIPZIG

as also the fact that he had always been somewhat envious, was not unknown to our Bach. With this, Reinken invited Bach to his house, and treated him with great courtesy.

In 1723 the town of Leipzig chose our Bach as their Director of Music and Cantor of St Thomas' School.[24] He accepted this invitation, although it was with reluctance that he left his gracious Prince. It seems as if Providence wished to remove him from Cöthen before the death of the Prince which, contrary to all expectation, took place shortly afterwards[25]; in this way he was at least no longer compelled to be actually present at this sad event. He had, however, the melancholy satisfaction of composing, while at Leipzig, the funeral music for his so dearly beloved Prince, and of performing it in person at Cöthen.

Not long after this, he was appointed Capellmeister to the Duke of Weissenfels; and in 1736 he was made Court Composer to the King of Poland and Elector of Saxony, having some time previously played the organ in public at Dresden, before the Court and the musical connoisseurs of the town, with great applause.[26]

In 1747 he visited Berlin, and it was on this occasion that he received the honour of playing before His Majesty the King of Prussia at Potsdam. His Majesty himself played over to him a theme for a fugue, which, to His Majesty's very great satisfaction, he immediately worked out on the pianoforte. Thereupon His Majesty expressed a desire to hear a fugue with six obbligato parts; and this command also he immediately carried out upon a theme of his own choice, to the wonder of the King and the musicians present. After his return to Leipzig he wrote out two Ricercars (so called), one in three parts, the other in six, together with certain other smaller works, all upon the theme given him by His Majesty; had them engraved upon copper, and dedicated them to the King.[27]

His sight, naturally somewhat weak, had been still further impaired by his unheard-of zeal for study, at which, especially in his youth, he would sit up all night; and the result was that in his last years his eyes

BACH'S LAST ILLNESS

became diseased. Partly from a desire to continue to serve God and his neighbour — his mental and bodily powers being otherwise still very brisk — and partly on the advice of certain friends, who put much faith in an eye-doctor who had just arrived in Leipzig, he wished to obtain relief by an operation. This, however, had to be repeated; and even so it turned out very badly. Not only did he not regain his sight; but also his health, otherwise extremely sound, was completely broken down by the operation and the injurious medicines and treatment associated with it; so that for fully six months thereafter he was nearly always unwell. Ten days before his death his eyes seemed suddenly to improve, so that one morning he could again see perfectly well, and bear the light. But a few hours later he was struck down with apoplexy; and upon this followed a high fever, of which, despite the utmost care of two of the most skilful doctors in Leipzig, he died quietly and peacefully at a quarter to nine in the evening of 28 July 1750, in his sixty-sixth year.[28]

PUBLISHED WORKS

OF THE WORKS for which we have to thank this great composer, the following have been made available to the public by their being engraved:

1 Clavierübung [Clavier Exercises], First Part: consisting of six Suites

2 Clavierübung, Second Part: consisting of a Concerto and an Overture for a two-manual clavicembalo

3 Clavierübung, Third Part: consisting

of a number of preludes on certain chorales, for organ

4 An Aria with Thirty Variations, for [a clavicembalo with] two manuals

5 Six three-part Preludes, for [vor] the same number of chorales, for organ

6 Certain Canonic Variations on the chorale VOM HIMMEL HOCH DA KOMM ICH HER

7 Two Fugues [Ricercars], a Trio, and a number of Canons, on the above-mentioned theme set by His Majesty the King of Prussia,

PUBLISHED WORKS

under the title of MUSICAL OFFERING

8 THE ART OF FUGUE. This, the composer's last work, contains Counterpoints [i.e. Fugues] and Canons of all kinds upon a single main theme. His last illness prevented him from finishing what was to have been, according to plan, the penultimate fugue, and from composing the final one, which was to have had four subjects, and afterwards to have been inverted note for note in all four parts. This work was not published until after the late composer's death.²⁹

The following is an approximate list of the late Bach's unpublished works:

1 Five annual cycles of Church Cantatas, for all Sundays and Feast-days

2 A number of Oratorios and Masses: a Magnificat: some settings of the Sanctus: Dramas, Serenades: music for birthdays, anniversaries, and funerals: music for weddings, and one or two comic Cantatas

3 Five Passions, of which one is for double choir

4 Some Motets for double choir

UNPUBLISHED WORKS

5 A large number of free Preludes, Fugues, and similar pieces, for the organ with obbligato pedal

6 Six Trios [Sonatas] for the organ with obbligato pedal

7 A number of Preludes for [vor] Chorales, for the organ

8 A book full of short Preludes for [vor] the majority of church hymns, for the organ

9 Two sets of Twenty-four Preludes and Fugues in all keys, for the clavier

10 Six Toccatas for the clavier

11 Six Suites ['English'] for the same

12 Six more of the same, somewhat shorter [the 'French' Suites]

13 Six Sonatas for Violin, without bass

14 Six of the same for Violoncello

15 Sundry concertos for one, two, three, and four clavicembalos

16 Finally, many other instrumental pieces, of all kinds, and for all instruments.³⁰

OUR BACH married twice. His first wife was Maria Barbara, youngest daughter of the

FIRST MARRIAGE

above-mentioned Johann Michael Bach, a noteworthy composer[31]. By her he had seven children, five sons and two daughters, among whom were a pair of twins. Three of them are still alive, namely: the eldest (unmarried) daughter, Catharina Dorothea, born in 1708: Wilhelm Friedemann, born in 1710, now Director of Music and Organist of the Market Church, Halle: and Carl Philipp Emanuel, born in 1714, Chamber-musician to the King of Prussia[32]. With this his first wife he enjoyed thirteen years of contented married life; but at Cöthen, in the year 1720, he was overtaken by sore affliction: on his return from a journey to Carlsbad with his Prince, he found her dead and buried, although at his departure he had left her hale and hearty. He heard nothing of her illness and death until he entered his house.

At Cöthen, in 1721, he took his second wife: Anna Magdalena, youngest daughter of Herr Johann Caspar Wikken, Court Trumpeter to the Duke of Weissenfels.[33] Of the thirteen children (six sons and seven daughters) whom she bore him, the following six are still

SECOND MARRIAGE

alive: 1, Gottfried Heinrich, born in 1724: 2, Elisabeth Juliane Fridrike, born in 1726; who is married to Herr Altnikol, organist of St. Wenceslas, Naumburg, and an able composer: 3, Johann Christoph Friedrich, born in 1732, now Chamber-musician to the High Count of the Empire [Wilhelm von] Schaumburg-Lippe: 4, Johann Christian, born in 1735: 5, Johanna Carolina, born in 1737: 6, Regina Susanna, born in 1742. The widow also is still alive.[34]

This is a very brief account of the life of a

man who proved a quite exceptional honour to music, his fatherland, and his family.

IF EVER A COMPOSER displayed the full power of polyphony, and made artistic use of the most hidden mysteries of harmony, then certainly our Bach did; none other has infused such imaginative and various life into these otherwise dry-seeming artifices. He had but to hear a theme to realize instantly how it could be subjected to artistic treatment. His melodies were certainly peculiar; but

COMPOSER & CONDUCTOR

always different, full of invention, and unlike those of any other composer. His serious temperament inclined him chiefly to laborious, serious, and profound music; yet he could also condescend, when necessary, to a light and jocular manner, especially in his playing. Constant practice in the composition of polyphonic works had given him so quick an eye that he could grasp, at a glance, all the simultaneously-sounding parts in the largest scores. His ear was so keen that even in the most complex music he was able to detect the slightest error; it was unfortunate that he seldom had the good fortune to find for his works performers such as might have spared him the necessity of making comments of this disagreeable kind. In conducting he was very accurate, and in his tempi (which he generally took very fast) extremely certain.

So long as nothing can be brought against us but the bare possibility that still better organists and clavier-players have existed, we cannot be blamed for being bold enough to assert, still, that our BACH WAS THE GREAT-

BACH AS PERFORMER

EST ORGANIST AND CLAVIER-PLAYER that has ever lived. No doubt many a famous man has done great things in polyphony on these instruments; but was he therefore just as skilful — and moreover, as skilful with hands and feet together — as our Bach[?]. Those who have had the pleasure of hearing him as well as other players, and who are not otherwise prejudiced, will consider this doubt not unfounded. And those who examine Bach's organ and clavier works — which, as is generally known, he himself performed without simplifications or omissions — will likewise find little to set against the above assertion. How strange, how novel, how expressive, how beautiful were his flights of fancy in extemporizing! how perfectly he expressed them! His fingers were all exercised alike: all were equally equipped to yield the utmost purity in performance. He had devised for himself a system of fingering so convenient that for him it was not hard to perform the most difficult passages with the most flowing ease. Before him, the most famous clavier-players in Germany and other countries had

BACH AND THE ORGAN 47

made little use of the thumb; he made all the better use of it. With his two feet he could play on the pedals passages that many a not unskilful clavier-player would have found hard enough with his five fingers. Not only did he understand the management of the organ to perfection: how most fitly to combine stops with each other, and how to show off each stop to the best effect, according to its character; he had also a thorough knowledge of organ-building. This latter he once made more than usually evident, at the examination of a new organ in the church near which his remains now rest. The builder of this organ was a man in the last years of his long life. The examination was perhaps one of the most rigorous ever made; consequently, the fact that Bach publicly expressed his complete satisfaction with the work by no means lessened the repute either of the organ-builder or — owing to certain circumstances — of Bach himself.[35]

No-one was better able than he to work out and criticize specifications for new organs. Despite all this knowledge of the organ, he

TUNING THE CLAVIER

was (as he would often complain) never so fortunate as to have a really large and fine organ for his own constant use. We have thus been deprived of many beautiful and unheard compositions for the organ[36], which otherwise he would have committed to paper and set forth just as he had them in his head. And, to omit other merits that were his[37], in tuning the clavicembalo he tempered it so purely and correctly that all keys sounded well and pleasantly. He knew of no key that had to be avoided because of incorrect tuning.

For his moral character they can speak who enjoyed his conversation and friendship, and are become witnesses to his integrity before God and his neighbour.

[38] He joined the Society of Musical Sciences in June 1747, at the suggestion of Court Councill or Mizler, whose good friend he was, and to whom, when still studying in Leipzig, he had given instruction in clavier-playing and composition. To be sure, our late Bach would have nothing to do with deep theoretical speculations about music; but he was all the stronger in

practical matters. He supplied the Society with the chorale VOM HIMMEL HOCH DA KOMM' ICH HER, completely worked out; it was afterwards engraved on copper. He had also submitted to the Society the Canon engraved on Tab. iv f. 16 [see p. 63][39], and would certainly have done much more had he not been prevented by lack of time; for he was a member of the Society for only three years.

The LIBRETTO in his honour as a member, composed in the Society's name by Herr Doctor Georg Venzky, reads thus:

THE NEKROLOG

CHORUS

O Muses, mute your strings!
Break off, break off your songs of joy! —
to contentment a limit is set —
and sing to comfort afflicted brethren.
Hear what [news] Report brings to you:
hear the lamentations of Leipzig.

    It will grieve you:
        yet must ye listen.

LEIPZIG

RECITATIVE OR NARRATIVE

The mighty Bach, who to our town —

WENZKY'S LIBRETTO

yea, to the wide realms of Europe —
brought renown, and made little of his powers,
is, alas! a corpse.
The Bach who our Academy
so incomparably adorned:
Bach, who with his delightful wit,
with the sound of his strings
and many kinds of song,
did children, men, and women —
yea, Princes, Kings, and all real connoisseurs —
enchant, teach, and affect:
He has now to trouble our repose;

THE NEKROLOG

he has died, and hasteneth to higher choirs.

ARIOSO

The faithful Bach is dead;
Music and organs are silenced.
O grief, O fall, O misery!
How our hearts bleed!

COMPOSERS OR MUSICIANS

ARIA

Whither hastenest thou, honourable Bach?
Dost thou fill thy guild with bitter woe and anguish?
Ah! shall thy melodies

WENZKY'S LIBRETTO

    no more uplift, delight us?
God let thy spirit on thy brethren rest,
that they may help their art to make progress
and magnify His majesty as it deserves.
To all of them we will render praise;
yet follows thee the longing cry:
Whither hastenest thou, honourable Bach?

THE FRIENDS OF MUSIC

NARRATIVE

How skilful, how accomplished
was the transfigured Bach,

THE NEKROLOG

so soon from us removed!
   How rich, how individual,
   how unfathomable was
   his noble spirit,
that has delivered itself from mortality!
   How manifold
   was his art,
which did not draw, but dragged to itself
perforce the favour of all connoisseurs!
His flight was high, his warmth of
              [imagination great,
   his praise charming,

WENZKY'S LIBRETTO

his blame caustic.
We ravished heard him magnify the Creator's fame.
His lamentation struck through ears and eyes and hearts:
his rejoicing lightened the heaviest grief.
Alas that we have lost this hero among virtuosos!
   Yet we shall find the more refreshment
   in the masterpieces
   that he has left us
   as a noble relic.

ARIOSO

Jehovah grant long life to the virtuosos
who are yet able to exalt the sweet art!

THE NEKROLOG

THE MUSICAL SOCIETY

TWO-PART ARIA

Wail, brethren, in emulation,
and lament our loss!
Our God has struck the door
so that the strongest pillars quake.
Let the tears run their course,
and therewith
let the merit of your Bach
be constantly heard in your choirs.
Alas that the oppressed breast
has breath to lament with!

WENZKY'S LIBRETTO

Wail, brethren, in emulation,
and lament our loss!

THE GLORIFIED ONE

NARRATIVE

Lament not, ye friends and connoisseurs;
fortune favours me yet.
Lament not, ye brethren and patrons:
cast but a glance upon these heights!
O could ye hear the beauteous strains
that our choir raises to the glory of God!
O could ye hear the music-making

THE NEKROLOG

that here has no ending!
O could ye learn the arts
that my soul has already learnt
since it departed from you!
Ye would take wings and fly
to this summit full of sweetness:
ye would wish my Muse God speed,
not [wish to?] drag it back.
Therefore take comfort
and follow me. What ye have lost in me
ye shall find, and better, within our gates.
Nought, nought is like these singers.

Therefore take comfort.

CHORUS

Ye dwellers in heaven, welcome with joy
the brother who adorned our arts;
and let us with most fervent united voices
sing to the laud, honour, and majesty of the Highest!
Who hopes and believes shall enter heaven's gate,
and, glorified, praise God in the angel-choir.
O Christ, help us, then, to do what is needful,
that we also may depart hence in Thy goodwill.

    Ye dwellers in heaven etc.

CANON

APPENDIX I

EXTRACT FROM

Musicalisches | LEXICON | Oder | Musicalische Bibliothec, | . . . . von Johann Gottfried Walthern, 4°. . . . Leipzig, 1732.

BACH (JOH. SEBASTIAN), son of Herr Joh. Ambrosius Bach, who became a Court and Town Musician at Eisenach; born there 21 March 1685; learnt the first principles of the clavier from his eldest brother Herr Johann Christoph Bach, who became organist and a member of the school staff at Ohrdruf; was organist first in 1703[41] of the New Church at Arnstadt, and in 1707 of the Church of St. Blasius, Mühlhausen; came[42] to Weimar in

1708, became here[42] Chamber Musician and Court Organist, and in 1714 Concertmeister, to the Duke; in 1717 Capellmeister to the Prince of Cöthen, and in 1723, after the death of the late Herr Kuhnau, Director of Music in Leipzig, and also Capellmeister to the Prince of Saxe-Weissenfels[43]. Of his admirable clavier works the following have been published [engraved] on copper : in 1726 a Partita in B flat major, under the title 'Clavier-Übung, consisting of Preludes, Allemands, Courantes, Sarabandes, Gigues,

Minuets, etc.' This has been followed by the second [Partita], in C minor, the third, in A minor, the fourth, in D major, the fifth, in G major, and the sixth, in E minor; with which the Opus is probably complete.⁴⁴

The Bach family are probably of Hungarian descent⁴⁵, and all that have borne this name have, so far as is known, been devoted to music; which is perhaps because even the letters b′a′c′h′ are melodic when taken in their order — a fact first remarked on by Herr Bach of Leipzig.⁴⁶

APPENDIX II

Extract from

THE BACH GENEALOGY[47]

No. 24. JOH. SEBASTIAN BACH, youngest son of Joh. Ambrosius Bach, was born at Eisenach on 21 March 1685. Became (1) Court Musician to Duke Johann Ernst of Weimar, anno 1703. (2) Organist of the New Church at Arnstadt, 1704.[48] (3) Organist of the Church of St. Blasius at Mühlhausen, anno 1707. (4) Chamber[49] and Court Organist at Weimar, anno 1708. (5) At the same Court, anno 1714, Concertmeister also. (6) Capellmeister and

Director of Chamber-music to the Princely Court of Anhalt-Cöthen, anno 1717. (7) Was called to Leipzig, anno 1723, as Director of Choral Music and Cantor of St. Thomas' School; where according to God's holy Will he lives yet to the present day, and functions also as honorary Capellmeister to Weissenfels and Cöthen⁵⁰. His family follows { from No. 45 to No. 57. Died 30 July⁵¹ 1750}

NOTES

The word CLAVIER is annoying to the translator. It means either MANUAL (of an organ or two-manual harpsichord) or ANY KEYBOARD INSTRUMENT, sometimes including the organ, but not always. Where it has the latter sense I have left it untranslated, and the reader must understand harpsichord (clavicembalo), clavichord, or organ, according to the context.

PAGE 2

'These remarks on the persistence of musical gifts in the Bach family are hardly exaggerated. At Erfurt the name was so strongly associated with music that a local musician would be called a Bach whether or no that was in fact his name. All Sebastian's sons were professional musicians, except Gottfried Heinrich (he was musical, but half-witted); so was his grandson Wilhelm Friedrich Ernst Bach, who died 25 Dec. 1845, the

TO PAGE 2

last male descendant of Sebastian Bach.

² From the Genealogy we learn that Veit Bach was a miller. The author of the Genealogy evidently knew nothing of his life before he left Hungary, and probably thought he was born there; in some such way arose, no doubt, the notion that the family was of Hungarian origin (see Appendix I). Actually, the name Bach is recorded in Thuringia from 1509 onwards. Terry suggests that Veit was born at Wechmar (the church there is dedicated to St. Vitus) and

wandered to Hungary in his youth.

At any rate, when he left Hungary (probably during the reign of the counter-Reformationist Rudolf II, 1576–1612) it was in Wechmar that he settled; and he died there 8 Mar. 1619. The Genealogy says, 'His greatest delight was a little zither, which he would take with him into the mill and play as the wheel went round. (It must have sounded well, the two of them! However, he thus taught himself to keep time.) And this, it seems, was the beginning of the musical gifts of his descendants.'

PAGE 6

[3] To judge from the organ chorale-preludes in Keller's collection of ancient works (Peters edition), two of these five parts must have been supplied by the imagination of Christoph's audiences.

PAGE 8

[4] For further information about the early Bachs see Grove and the major works on Sebastian.

[5] The Nekrolog, Walther, and the Genealogy agree on this date. It is Old Style. The Eisenach

registers (facsimile in H. Reimann, Johann Sebastian Bach, Zweite Auflage, ... erweitert von Bruno Schrader. Berlin [1921]) do not record Bach's birth, but only his baptism on March 23: two days later, as the custom was.

⁶ Ambrosius was born 22 Feb. 1645, and died 31 Jan 1695. He married Elisabeth Lämmerhirt, daughter of a furrier, on 8 Ap. 1668. Elisabeth was born 24 Feb. 1644, and died 3 May 1694.

⁷ This Christoph died in 1693.

PAGE 9

[8] Christoph was born in 1671. He had received lessons from the well-known organist and composer Johann Pachelbel, who stood godfather to his sister Johanna Juditha Bach, born in 1680.

PAGE 12

[9] Emanuel and Agricola evidently thought that Christoph died in 1699 or 1700. Actually he lived until 1721.

PAGE 13

[10] The words 'In the year 1700' are a correction.

The original has 'After his brother's death'. See note 9.

Since Sebastian's arrival in Ohrdruf in 1695, Christoph had had two or three children born to him; and it would seem that by 1700 there was no room in the house for Sebastian. The Ohrdruf school register records that Bach left on 15 Mar. 1700 'ob defectum hospitiorum'. There is a precisely similar entry concerning Erdmann on 19 Jan. 1700.

Lüneburg was a long way off, and the boys must have had some reason for going there; it

TO PAGES 13-14   87

is reasonable to suppose that they were recommended to the authorities at Lüneburg by one Elias Herder, who had been educated there before coming to ~~Lüneburg~~ Ohrdruf as a master in 1697. Both boys were at Lüneburg for Easter 1700 (April 3).

Erdmann and Bach kept in touch until 1730 at least; in that year Bach sent to his old schoolfellow an important letter that will be referred to later.

PAGE 14

"Little is known of Bach's schooldays apart

from the account given here. From the registers of both schools it can be deduced that he made good progress in his studies; he received a sound general education, including Latin.

The well-known anecdote of Bach's finding money in two herring-heads, which fell at his feet as he sat sniffing hungrily outside a wayside hostelry (Marpurg, Legende einiger Musikheiligen, 1786), refers to one of these journeys to Hamburg.

Hamburg was thirty miles from Lüneburg, Celle sixty. The Nekrolog is too much concerned with Bach's 'unheard-of zeal for study', and the long journeys he accordingly undertook in order to hear Reinken and the band at Celle, to mention Georg Böhm, who was on his doorstep at St. John's, Lüneburg. Böhm was a Thuringian and a pupil of Reinken's. His characteristic style seems to be reflected in Bach's early Chorale-Partitas and certain other works.

PAGE 15

[12] It must have been at this time that Bach competed for the organistship of the Market Church,

NOTE 12

Sangerhausen. This post fell vacant in 1702 (July 3). In 1736 another vacancy occurred; and Bach wrote to one J. F. Klemm, a Councillor at Sangerhausen, recommending his son Johann Gottfried Bernhard for the post (see note 25). [p.173] In his second letter to Klemm, dated 18 Nov. 1736, Bach refers to his having been a candidate for the same post thirty years before, and having 'obtained the vote', although 'the higher powers' caused another candidate to be appointed. 'The higher powers' must have been the Duke of Weissenfels, lord of the town;

TO PAGE 15

the successful candidate was one Kobelius, whose grandfather had been Court Organist at Weissenfels. The courts of Weissenfels and Weimar were on friendly terms; Bach's appointment to Weimar may have been arranged as a compensation for his failure at Sangerhausen. However this may be, Easter Day (April 8) 1703 found him installed in the chamber orchestra maintained by Duke Johann Ernst of Weimar.

This Duke is not to be confused with his elder brother, whom Bach served from 1708 to 1717. See note 22, p.113.

PAGE 15

[13] On 7 Aug. 1581, a very hot day, one Hans Nebel of Arnstadt saw fit to tar his roof. A neighbour who pointed out the danger of fire was told to go to the devil; whereupon the latter did his stuff. The ensuing conflagration involved the church of St. Boniface, which was not rebuilt until 1676-83.

The organ, naturally, was newer than the church. It was not finished until the beginning of July 1703; and was then examined by experts, of whom Bach (aged 18) was one.

TO PAGE 15   93

His expenses were paid on July 13, and in the document concerning this payment he is referred to as Court Organist to the Duke of Weimar. In reality, one Effler seems to have held that post; but it may be supposed that Bach, officially a string-player in Duke Johann Ernst's band, had played upon the organ in the chapel attached to the Court of the reigning Duke, Wilhelm Ernst. In any case, it is clear that he already had a reputation as an organist.

Bach opened the organ, presumably on one

of the Sundays in July.' The minute of his appointment as organist is dated 9 Aug. 1703; his formal induction (durch Handschlag) took place on Aug. 14.

The words 'Later in the same year' are a correction. The Nekrolog reads 'Das Jahr drauf' (In the following year), thus dating the appointment 1704, as the Genealogy does expressly.

PAGE 16

¹⁴ The subject of the Passacaglia is said to owe something to one André Raison. There is an article on Bach's borrowings from the French

TO PAGES 15–16   95

in the Bach-Jahrbuch for 1910.

[15] This was in October 1705. The distance is 300 miles; it is not surprising that Bach overstayed his leave and consequently fell into trouble with his pastors and masters. The latter undoubtedly had just cause for complaint, quite apart from his late return on this occasion. Bach had a hasty temper, it would seem; he was an indifferent organizer, and at no time did he show any sympathy with the unmusical. He therefore made a poor choirmaster. In addition, his

extemporized preludes to the hymn-verses failed
to give satisfaction; it was said that they had
been too long, and their harmony extravagant,
and that when he was asked to shorten and
simplify them, he promptly made them too short.
(He was a true organist! One is reminded of
Samuel Sebastian Wesley, of whom it is said
that he was sacked by one of those Deans with
whom he was perpetually at war, but reinstated
by the Bishop; whereupon he played for his
next voluntary 'Fixed in His everlasting seat'.)
Finally, he was questioned about his introducing

TO PAGE 16.

'a stranger maiden' into the church. It is supposed that this was Maria Barbara Bach, his cousin and first wife, and that he brought her to the church to sing to his accompaniment (not, of course, at services).

At Arnstadt Bach wrote the 'Capriccio on the Departure of his beloved Brother', a piece of programme music (for clavier) modelled on the Biblical Sonatas of Kuhnau (David and Goliath, etc.), and inspired by his brother Johann Jakob's removal to Sweden in 1704.

Terry gives a photograph and a careful

specification of the Arnstadt organ, whose console is still in existence. The pedalboard had a compass extending from CC to d', but lacking CC sharp: an arrangement not unusual at that date.

[16] Bach was appointed on 15 June 1707, and probably began his duties on Sept. 15. At Mühlhausen he married for the first time; see p. 38. Here also he drew up a specification of the work to be done on his organ, which was to be rebuilt. Much has been made of his inclusion

TO PAGE 16

of a pedal glockenspiel and of his demand that the tremulant should be put in order; it has not been so much emphasized that the glockenspiel was asked for and paid for by the parishioners, and that the tremulant had to be put right whether Bach intended to use it or not.

The glockenspiel was to have had twenty-six bells. This gives us the compass of the pedal-board: CC to d', without CC sharp, as at Arnstadt.

The rebuilding of the organ was not completed until 1709, after Bach's removal to

Weimar; but he gave the opening recital. This apparently took place on the Reformation Festival, an occasion for which the chorale 'Ein' feste Burg' was appropriate. Bach's solitary prelude on this chorale was copied by J.G. Walther, who marked registration such as Bach might have used at Mühlhausen to show off the new stops he had specified; and it may be supposed that he played the prelude on that occasion. Whether he composed it specially, or was merely using an old favourite of the congregation's, is unknown.

PAGE 17

'7 Bach's letter of resignation is dated 25 June 1708. In it he speaks of his not having been allowed to do his work without opposition from his own congregation, and says that this opposition shows no sign of abating. It is possible, too, that he became involved in a theological controversy that was then agitating the town.

His exact position at Weimar when he first went there is not known. In the above-mentioned letter he refers to his appointment to the 'Hof Capelle und Cammer Music' (as Terry puts it, to 'the Duke's general musical establishment and the select body of string players who performed in his private apartments'.) In the Genealogy he is described as 'Cammer und Hoforganist in Weimar, An. 1708'. Walther says he was at first 'Cammer- Musicus und Hof-Organist'. Certainly he was Court Organist by 1710; in the financial year Michaelmas 1710 – Michaelmas 1711 he received an allowance for the heating of the organ chamber in the Court chapel. There is no record of what happened to his predecessor Johann Effler. Most probably

TO PAGE 17

Bach took over the organist's duties as soon as he arrived.

The specification of the organ is given in Gottfried Albin Wette's 'Historische Nachrichten von der berühmten Residenz-Stadt Weimar' (Weimar, 1737). If I remember rightly, Wette includes a glockenspiel, which is omitted from Terry's quotation (p. 97 of the Biography). But I may be quite wrong. In any case, the glockenspiel was added between Michaelmas 1715 and 1716; and this is the most satisfactory piece of evidence for Bach's reputed interest in these devices — so far as I have been able to discover.

About this time Bach seems to have had access to an organ with an e′ pedalboard, though he did not use that note frequently. It will be found in the Fugue à la Gigue, the early Prelude and Fugue in G, the Prelude and Fugue in A, and the Second Concerto. The last-named work was almost certainly produced at Weimar, before the death (in 1715) of the young Duke Johann Ernst, for whom Walther made a number of similar arrangements.ˣ I suspect,

ˣ Bach's four Concertos are not original works.

TO PAGE 17   105

therefore, that the organ for which Bach wrote these high pedal parts was either his own or that in the Town Church, where Walther was organist; unless, indeed, these works were composed for a pedal harpsichord, which seems unlikely.

[18] There is no reason to question the Nekrolog's statement that Bach composed most of his organ works at Weimar; but a reservation must be made: the works as we know them may be products of elaborate later revision. For instance,

NOTES 18 – 20

the early versions of the Eighteen Chorale-preludes probably date from Weimar; but the revised versions familiar to us were made after 1730.

PAGE 18

[19] The appointment dates from Mar. 2; and one of the duties was to produce new Cantatas monthly.

PAGE 19

[20] F. W. Zachau, Handel's master, died in Aug. 1712. Bach visited Halle late in 1713, and was perhaps attracted by the organ then under construction in the Markt- or Liebfrauenkirche.

TO PAGES 17–19

The post being vacant, he performed a 'test-piece' there — probably Cantata 21. He returned to Weimar, where he received an invitation to Halle (the letter is dated Dec. 14). Bach was not altogether satisfied with the conditions of the appointment; and what with this and the Duke's unwillingness to let him go, it would seem that the matter remained unsettled until Bach's appointment as Concertmeister at Weimar (Mar. 2, 1714) caused him to refuse the Halle post. Some of the correspondence has been lost; but from Bach's letter of March 19 it is evident that he had been accused of using the invitation to Halle as a means of extorting promotion at Weimar.

At some unknown date between Michaelmas 1714 and Michaelmas 1715 Bach had an accident for which he received twelve florins compensation. In 1714 (perhaps during his convalescence? but it seems unlikely) he found leisure for the lengthy task of copying Frescobaldi's 'Fiori musicali' — 104 pages of MS.

It would seem that it was late in 1714

TO PAGE 19

(after Sept. 7) that Bach visited Cassel for some unknown reason and received from the Hereditary Prince Friedrich a ring, as reward for his virtuosity on the pedals. 'His feet, flying over the pedals as though they were winged, made the notes reverberate like thunder in a storm,' wrote Constantin Bellermann, continuing: 'if Bach's skilful feet deserved such a bounty, what gift must the Prince have offered to reward his hands as well?' (Programma in quo Parnassus Musarum, etc. (1743); tr. Terry. See also Adlung's Anleitung (1758), p. 690: and an article by Carl Scherer in Monats. f. Musik-geschichte, Jahrg. 25, p. 129.)

At Weimar Bach was intimate with J. G. Walther (p. 219), and presumably made the acquaintance of J. M. Gesner, who became Conrector at the Gymnasium in 1715. They met again at Leipzig in 1730.

In 1716 Bach attended his master on a visit to Weissenfels, and performed his secular Cantata 'Was mir behagt' there on the Duke's birthday (Feb. 23). Shortly afterwards (Ap. 20) he was invited to report on the new organ at

TO PAGES 19 & 24

Halle that had (perhaps) attracted him two years before. The examination took place on April 29 and 30; and on Sunday May 3 the organ was opened. A banquet followed, whose appalling menu (still preserved) justifies Terry's remark: 'Little wonder that a big blot fell on the 'Bach' as the writer signed a receipt for six thalers, his fee!'

PAGE 24

[21] Marchand was born in 1669 and died in 1732. There are several accounts of the contest, which differ a good deal in detail. It seems

curious, to say the least of it, that Bach should have been specially invited to Dresden by Jean-Baptiste Volumier (obviously a Frenchman) in order to discredit another Frenchman; and perhaps Terry is right in suggesting that Bach visited Dresden in order to hear Marchand, the contest being arranged afterwards. It took place about September. There is no evidence that Bach was deprived of a present from the King, or even that any such present was ever spoken of.

TO PAGE 24

22 The story of Bach's removal to Cöthen begins with his relations with the Dukes of Weimar.

When he first went to Weimar in 1703, it was to serve Duke Johann Ernst. In 1708 his employer was Duke Wilhelm Ernst, elder brother of Johann, who, meanwhile, had died in 1707. The brothers had been on bad terms.

Wilhelm was childless; Johann had two sons, Ernst August and Johann Ernst. The former came of age in 1709, and got on with his uncle no better than his father had done. He was a pupil of Bach's, as was also his brother Johann Ernst the younger, who died in 1715; and Bach was evidently on intimate terms with this side of the family, for Ernst August's wife stood godmother to a short-lived son of Bach's born at Cöthen in 1718.

In Bach's last years at Weimar relations between Wilhelm Ernst and Ernst August became so bad that the former forbade members of his Capelle (among others) to visit his nephew's court. Bach must have found the situation difficult. Further, on 1 Dec. 1716 the senile Capellmeister at Weimar (one Drese) died;

TO PAGE 24   115

and Bach had reason to be annoyed when the vacancy was filled by Drese's son, who does not seem to have been particularly competent, instead of by himself, who since his appointment as Concertmeister in March 1714 had been fulfilling one of the Capellmeister's most important duties: the composition of Cantatas (monthly).

On 24 Jan. 1716 Ernst August had married Eleonore, sister of Prince Leopold of Anhalt-Cöthen; and it was, no doubt, as a result of Bach's intimacy with his sister's husband that Leopold offered him the Capellmeistership at Cöthen. He accepted, and was formally appointed on 5 Aug. 1717; but Wilhelm Ernst refused to allow him to go; no doubt he was incensed by Bach's intimacy with his nephew, and by that nephew's (presumable) assistance in obtaining Bach his new post. After the contest with Marchand Bach probably felt that now was the time to press for his release; at all events, he did so, to such purpose that on Nov. 6 he was imprisoned for his obstinacy. He was released on Dec. 2 'with a grudging permission,' says the Court Secretary, 'to retire from the Duke's service.'

TO PAGE 24

(Emanuel and Agricola perhaps thought it as well to draw a decent veil over this incident.) By Dec. 10 he was settled in Cöthen; his family may have moved in before that date.

With his departure from Weimar Bach ceased to be a professional organist. At Cöthen it was not his duty to play at all, but to conduct and provide music for the Prince's band. On what organ he kept up his technique we do not know. There were three available: in the Schloss chapel a two-manual of thirteen stops (the Prince did not maintain an organist of his own; he was

NOTE 22

a Calvinist, and no elaborate music was performed in his chapel): at St. James' (also a Calvinist church) a fairly large organ: and at St. Agnes' a small organ with an f' sharp pedalboard — for which there is no particular reason to suppose that the Orgelbüchlein preludes on 'Gottes Sohn' and 'In dulci jubilo' were originally composed.

According to Bach, Prince Leopold (born in 1694) 'loved and understood music' (letter to Erdmann). Certainly he seems to have been much attached to his gifted Capellmeister, whose salary

TO PAGE 24

he made equal to that of the Hofmarschall, the second highest of the Court functionaries.

Bach had hardly arrived in Cöthen when he was invited to Leipzig to examine a new organ by Johann Scheibe, in St. Paul's Church. His report is dated 17 Dec. 1717. There is reason to believe that while in Leipzig he performed Cantata 61, at either St. Thomas' or St. Nicholas' (the cantata had had its first performance at Weimar in 1714).

In May 1718 Bach, with five other members of the Capelle and a clavicembalo, accompanied

Leopold to Carlsbad. They were back in Cöthen by June. On Nov. 17 the Prince and his younger brother stood godfathers to the last of Bach's children by his first wife (Leopold Augustus, b. 15 Nov.; buried 28 Sept. 1719). It was this child to whom Leopold's sister the Duchess Eleonore stood godmother.

In May 1720 Bach again visited Carlsbad with the Prince. They returned in July to find Maria Barbara dead and already buried (p. 40).

PAGE 25

[23] So the *Nekrolog*. The year was 1720, and the month (probably) October. The circumstances of Bach's visit are obscure; but Terry is perhaps right in supposing that he went there to inquire about the vacancy at St. James' caused by the death of Heinrich Friese on 12 Sept. 1720. On 21 Nov. the church authorities decided to invite eight men to compete for the post on Nov. 28; Bach was one of those named. Leopold's birthday fell on Nov. 29; and as musical celebrations were expected, Bach would have been unable

to remain in Hamburg for the competition. Furthermore, it was a rule, and well known, that the successful candidate would be expected to contribute to the church funds; and this may have deterred him. He played to Reinken (1623–1722), no doubt; but for the presence of 'the Magistracy and many other notables' we have only the Nekrolog's evidence.

The 'Great' G minor and the two preludes on 'An Wasserflüssen Babylon' are commonly associated with this occasion.

The successful candidate was one Heitmann;

TO PAGE 25

his appointment cost him 4000 marks. The pastor, Erdmann Neumeister (a well-known compiler of Cantata libretti, some of which were used by Bach) had perhaps hoped that Bach would be appointed; and shortly afterwards, in a sermon on the Christmas gospel, he said that if an angel from heaven had competed for the post, he would have been rejected unless he had brought money with him (Mattheson, *Der musicalische Patriot*, Hamburg 1728, p. 316).

On 24 March 1721 Bach wrote the dedicatory note of the Brandenburg Concertos, from which it is evident that these works had been commissioned 'two years ago'; it does not appear that they were either acknowledged or performed. Bach's second marriage took place on 3 Dec. 1721 (p. 40). Eight days later (Dec. 11) Leopold, in whose service Bach had expected to end his days, married (in Bach's words) 'a Bernburg wife, and in consequence, as it seemed, his musical inclination abated, while his new Princess proved to be an amusa. So it pleased God to call me here [Leipzig] as director Musices and Cantor of the Thomasschule. At

TO PAGE 25

first I found it not altogether agreeable to become a simple Cantor after having been a Capellmeister, and for that reason I forbore from coming to a *resolution* for three months. However, I received such *favorable* reports of the *situation*, that, having particularly in mind my sons' *studia*, and after invoking divine guidance, I at last made up my mind, came to Leipzig, performed my *Probe*, and received the post' (letter to Erdmann, tr. Terry. Italics — the underlining — indicate non-German words).

PAGE 27

[24] Johann Kuhnau, Cantor of the Thomas-schule since 1701, died on 5 June 1722. Of the six candidates for the vacancy who were under consideration on July 14, by far the most notable was G.P. Telemann (one of Emanuel Bach's godfathers); he was offered the post, and accepted. Things had gone so far by Aug. 14. Telemann, however, simply made use of his appointment to extort an increase of salary from his employers at Hamburg; and about the end of October he refused the Cantorate.

TO PAGE 27   127

Bach did not appear as a candidate until between Nov. 23 and Dec. 21; of the five men under consideration on the latter date, he and Graupner (of Darmstadt) were regarded as the most hopeful; and the latter was preferred. He was in charge of the music from Christmas until mid-January, and would have been appointed had not his master increased his salary. In the end he withdrew, in a letter dated 23 March 1723. Meanwhile Bach had performed Cantata 22 as his test-piece on Feb. 7 (Quinquagesima); and, presumably because no-one else was available, he was responsible for the Passion Music at St. Thomas' on Good Friday, March 26. So the St. John Passion had its first performance.

On April 4 Prince Leopold's wife died — too late. The Leipzig Council considered Graupner's withdrawal on April 9; Bach obtained his release from Cöthen on the 13th; and on the 22nd his appointment was agreed upon. On May 5 he signed a bond defining his duties; on the 30th he performed Cantata 75; and on June 1 he was formally inducted to

TO PAGE 27

the school. There he remained until his death twenty-seven years later.

One thinks of Bach as an organist; and it is curious to find that that was his profession for fourteen years only (1703-1717). After his six years' dalliance with secular music at Cöthen, he returned to the Church indeed, and for good; but not as an organist. His pastors and masters expected him to compose and conduct music for the churches of St. Thomas and St. Nicholas, to train his choirs, and in addition to teach non-musical subjects in the school, perform sundry disciplinary duties, and generally do what he was told. They got more (or perhaps it would be more correct to say, less) than they expected. Bach soon chose for his favourite title 'Director Musices'; and on composition and 'direction' (conducting) he concentrated; school duties and even choir-training were tasks that he found irksome, and he fairly soon found (legitimate) means of evading them. This does not mean that he was lazy. There is no reason to disbelieve the Nekrolog's statement (p.36) that he composed five cycles

TO PAGE 27

of Cantatas for the Sundays and festivals of the ecclesiastical year: 295 in all. Of these he had composed about thirty before he went to Leipzig; the rest were produced between 1723 and about 1744 — on the average, about one a month (cf. his duties as Concertmeister at Weimar, note 19, p. 106).

It was not long before the Leipzig authorities had a taste of the new Cantor's quality: For instrumentalists (it must be remembered that the weekly Cantatas had orchestral accompaniments) the Cantors had to depend on what they could pick up from various sources; in particular, from among the University students. The University had a church of its own — St. Paul's; before 1710, regular services were not held there, but the occasional festival services were taken by Kuhnau. This duty was known as the Old Service; and for performing it Kuhnau received a small salary. But in 1710 regular Sunday services were begun. The University authorities did not wish it to be thought that S. Paul's went with the Cantorate of St. Thomas' of necessity; and Kuhnau was only able to retain office,

TO PAGE 27

and with it his valuable connection with the student-instrumentalists, by undertaking to be responsible for the Sunday services (the 'New Service') as well as for the Old Service, without any increase in his salary. When Telemann was appointed Cantor in 1722 he obtained the University post as well; but he was plainly told that he received it on his merits, and not simply because he was Cantor of St. Thomas'.

During the interregnum that followed Kuhnau's death the duties at St. Paul's were performed by the organist of St. Nicholas', Johann Gottlieb Görner. When it became evident that there was a chance of Graupner's not being released from Darmstadt, Görner applied to be formally appointed; and on 3 April 1723 he became responsible for both Old and New Services. (Bach's appointment to St. Thomas' was agreed upon on the 22nd.)

At Michaelmas 1723 Bach demanded the salary due to him for the Old Service. (Of course, he had not performed these duties; he was merely asserting his right, as Cantor, to

TO PAGE 27

direct the Old Service. He maintained that the University had had no business to attempt to break in 1710, the old-established association.) After some argument it was agreed that the post was his; but it was not until later that he contrived to extort from the authorities even half his proper salary; and even after two years of controversy he could get no further. Accordingly, he appealed to the King (Augustus II, Elector of Saxony). After investigation the Elector gave his decision (21 Jan. 1726): Bach was to be responsible for the Old Service, and to receive the proper salary; the New Service was at the University's disposal. No provision was made for such non-recurrent occasions as public mournings; whence arose further trouble in 1727 (see below, p.139; further details in B.J. 1925).

Meanwhile, on 2 Nov. 1723 Bach had taken his choir to Störmthal to open an organ by Zacharias Hildebrand; and at Vespers on Christmas Day ne performed the Latin Magnificat.

For the Passion Music of 1724 Bach repeated the St. John. It was customary that a work should

TO PAGE 27   137

have its first performance at St. Thomas', but be repeated the following year at St. Nicholas'. Bach found the conditions at the latter church unsatisfactory, and issued programmes announcing a performance at St. Thomas'; but the Council agreed to repair St. Nicholas' clavier and adapt the choir gallery to his requirements, so he recalled his programmes.

On 25 June 1724 Bach, described as 'der berühmter Cantor und Capellmeister', opened a new organ at the church of St. Johannes and St. Salvator, Gera. In July, (1724) and again in Dec.

1725, he and his wife were paid for visits to Cöthen. It was in 1725 that Bach first set texts by 'Picander' (Christian Friedrich Henrici), a facile hack-writer whose rather tasteless productions frequently served Bach in later years.

A funeral on 4 Feb. 1726 was probably the occasion for which the magnificent motet 'Be not afraid' was composed. This year also saw the appearance of the first Partita, engraved and published 'in Verlegung des Autoris'; it was dedicated to the short-lived infant son of

TO PAGE 27

Prince Leopold, who had married for the second time in 1725. Nov. 30 was the new Princess' birthday; and Bach visited Cöthen to perform the cantata 'Steigt freudig in die Luft' in her honour.

On 6 Sept. 1727 the wife of the Elector died, and Saxony went into mourning for four months. Hans von Kirchbach, a young nobleman studying at the University, arranged for the delivery (by himself) of a funeral Oration in St. Paul's, with accompanying music which he commissioned Bach to write. The University students had already

NOTE 24

given Bach, rather than Görner, one or two commissions for semi-official functions organized by themselves; but the Oration was to be a formal University affair; and as the Elector's decision of 1726 took no account of such occasions, Görner thought it worth his while to assert his claim to compose the music — and receive the fee.

The Oration was to take place on Oct. 17. On the 9th the University authorities told Kirchbach that Bach must take no part in the ceremony. Kirchbach replied that it was too

TO PAGE 27

late; Bach had been paid, and had already written some of the music. Then the University said that Bach might compose the music, but Görner must perform it. Kirchbach took no notice of this. On Oct. 11 Görner told the Council that he must know where he stood. They sent immediately to Kirchbach, repeating their former message in peremptory terms. Kirchbach said at first that if he were further pestered he would cancel the whole thing; but later agreed to meet Görner, and in the end offered him twelve thalers to stand down. Görner accepted; but produced a document to be signed by Bach, binding the latter to keep out of any such ceremonies in the future. Next day (Oct. 12) the University Clerk took the document to Bach for his signature; his report was, 'I did my best from 11 to 12, but without success.' Bach never did sign. He finished the music on the 15th, and on the 17th conducted it, 'fixed in his everlasting seat' at the clavier in the gallery (B.J. 1925; Bitter ii, 9 and Sicul, Das thränende Leipzig, 1727).

In 1728 there was a minor controversy, which

TO PAGE 27

seems to have been decided in Bach's favour, about his right to choose the hymns before and after the sermon.

PAGE 27

25 Leopold died 19 Nov. 1728; Bach's Trauer-Music was performed at Cöthen on 24 March 1729. Part of this work, which has been lost, consisted of movements from the St. Matthew Passion fitted to new words by Picander.

The Passion itself had its first performance on Good Friday (April 15) 1729. Gerber, a pupil of Bach's, wrote (three years later): 'Some high officials and well-born ladies in one of the galleries began to sing the first Chorale with great devotion from their books. But as the theatrical music proceeded, they were thrown into the greatest wonderment, saying to each other, "What does it all mean?" while one old lady, a widow, exclaimed, "God help us! 'tis surely an Opera-comedy!"' (Bitter ii, 58; tr. Terry.)

On 16 Oct. 1729 Johann Heinrich Ernesti, Rector of the Thomasschule, died. He had been Rector since 1684, and thus must have been an old man at his death; I cannot at present

TO PAGE 27   145

find the date of his birth. In his later years he had grown slack, and the school had suffered accordingly; but Bach and he had been on good terms: his wife and daughter had stood as godmothers to two of Bach's children. For the memorial service Bach wrote the motet 'Der Geist hilft unser Schwachheit auf'.

The new Rector was not appointed until 8 June 1730; the choice was a fortunate one for Bach — Johann Matthias Gesner, who had probably known Bach at Weimar (p. 110), and greatly admired him. In his edition of Quintilian's

'Institutiones Oratoriae' Gesner comments at length on his author's remarks about a lyre-player, concluding 'I'm an honest admirer of your ancient world, but I tell you this Bach of mine, or another, if you can find one like him, is worth any number of Orpheuses, and twenty singers like Arion.'

How far Bach's contemporaries were able to appreciate his compositions is made all too clear by the widow's opinion of the St. Matthew Passion, quoted above; and the Leipzig Council — made up, no doubt, like other such bodies,

TO PAGE 27　　　　　　　　　　147

of persons even less musical than that horrified old lady — saw in the change of Rector an opportunity of getting rid of their troublesome Cantor. At a meeting on 2 Aug. 1730 they complained of his frequent absences from Leipzig (under the bond he had signed in 1723 he was supposed to ask permission whenever he wished to leave the town; but apparently he never did); and Hofrath Adrian Steger summed up by saying that the Cantor 'does nothing, refuses to explain his conduct, and neglects his singing lessons, not to mention other instances of his unsatisfactoriness.' Syndicus Job added that Bach was 'incorrigible'; and they decided to stop his salary.

This did not ~~so~~ affect what Bach called his 'accidentia' — the fees for funerals and weddings that made up the greater part of his income; but, needless to say, it stirred him to action. He retorted in a letter dated Aug. 23, maintaining (in language whose extreme simplicity shows exactly what he thought of the Council) that the faults of his choir and orchestra were due not to him, but to the admission into the school (against his

TO PAGE 27   149

recommendation) of unmusical boys, to the disappearance of 'the occasional **beneficia** which used to find their way into the pockets of 'the University student-instrumentalists (from whom the orchestra was to a large extent recruited), and to other causes beyond his control.

The Council did nothing more; and Bach ignored them, except that on 28 Oct. 1730 he wrote that important letter to Erdmann which has been previously referred to. He wrote: '(1) this situation is not as good as it was represented to be, (2) various *accidentia* relative to my station have been withdrawn, (3) living is expensive, and (4) my masters are strange folk with very little care for music in them. Consequently, I am subjected to constant annoyance, jealousy, and persecution. It is therefore in my mind, with God's assistance, to seek my fortune elsewhere. If your Honour [his schoolmate!] knows of or should hear of a *convenable* station in your town [Danzig], I beg you to let me have your valuable *recommendation*.' He goes on to give details of his present income:

TO PAGE 27

'if the death-rate is higher than <u>ordinairement</u>, my <u>accidentia</u> increase in proportion; but Leipzig is a healthy place, and for the past year, as it happens, I have received about 100 Kronen [one seventh of his total income] less than usual in funeral <u>accidentia</u>.'

Nothing came of this letter. Gesner was already in office; and he soon took care to make Bach's life easier, in more ways than one. At the reopening of the school (5 June 1732) after its enlargement, new rules were issued, in which Gesner's interest in the musical side of the school's work is made evident.

Forkel or somebody has recorded Bach's taking his eldest son, Wilhelm Friedemann, to the opera in Dresden; he would say, 'Shall we go and hear the pretty tunes?', or words to that effect. He was apparently friendly with J. A. Hasse, Capellmeister to the Electoral Court at Dresden; and was present at the first performance of Hasse's opera 'Cleofide' (13 Sept. 1731. See M. Falck, Wilhelm Friedemann Bach (1919), p. 10). Next day he gave a recital at St. Sophia's, in the presence of Hasse and other personages.

TO PAGE 27

His playing inspired some quasi-poetry (Bitter, ii, 157, and Terry, 211). It was seven years since his last recital, so far as we know (B.J. 1925, p.93); but now in February 1732 he played at Stöntzsch (Neue Sächsische Kirchengalerie, Bd. XV. Die Ephorie Borna. Hrsg. von den Geistlichen der Ephorie, p. 1091); and in Sept. 1732 he revisited Cassel, to report on the enlarged organ in St. Martin's. He and Anna Magdalena arrived on 21 Sept. 1732, and the organ was opened on Sunday the 28th (authorities given in Terry's footnotes to pp. 211-2).

NOTE 25

On 1 Feb. 1733 the Elector died, and Saxony went into mourning until July. This meant that no Cantatas were required for the churches, and Bach had leisure for another occupation. That he liked the title of Capellmeister is evident from his letter to Erdmann (p. 125); and not only did he value a Court appointment for its own sake: he also thought (see below) that it might serve to protect him against the 'annoyance, jealousy, and persecution' that beset him at Leipzig. As the post of Electoral Capellmeister was held by his friend Hasse, he decided to try to obtain

TO PAGE 27

an appointment as Court Composer; and as the Elector was a Roman Catholic, and a secular work perhaps seemed an inappropriate offering during a period of public mourning, he chose to make his diploma-piece a setting of the Kyrie and Gloria (the Lutheran Missa) — texts common to Catholics and Lutherans. This was the beginning of the B minor Mass.

The Missa was finished by the summer of 1733. In June the post of organist at St. Sophia's, Dresden, fell vacant; and on the 7th Bach drafted an application on behalf of his son Friedemann.

NOTE 25

The latter was heard on June 22, and appointed forthwith. He received the organ key on July 11, examined the organ, and began his duties on Aug. 1. Bach must have stayed with him in Dresden for at least part of this time; for the dedicatory letter that accompanied the Missa to the Court is addressed from Dresden and dated July 27. In this letter Bach speaks of his having been 'constantly exposed to undeserved affronts, even the confiscation of the *accidentia* due to me, annoyances not likely to recur should your Majesty be pleased to admit me to your Capella.'

TO PAGE 27   157

Unfortunately for Bach, the Elector was at this time much concerned with the situation in Poland, where a Nationalist movement, not quelled until the summer of 1734, was on foot. He turned a deaf ear not only to Bach's petition, but also to the series of congratulatory works that Bach and his Collegium Musicum performed in Leipzig on 3 Aug. 1733, his birthday: 5 September, his son's birthday: 8 December, the birthday of the Queen-Electress: 17 Jan. 1734, the coronation of the Elector and his Queen at Cracow: 3 August, his birthday: 5

October, the anniversary of his election to the throne of Poland (next day died Gottfried Reiche, trumpeter, of a stroke attributed to his exertions on the previous evening in an atmosphere of torch-smoke): and 7 October, his birthday (I have followed Terry, although he seems to give the Elector two birthdays). The works produced on these occasions were for the most part adaptations of material already available, including the Hosanna of the Mass (5 Oct. 1734) and parts of the Christmas Oratorio, which latter was performed as a whole in 1734.

TO PAGE 27

Bach's intensive cultivation of his sovereign ceased with the cantata performed on 7 Oct. 1734; and we hear no more of his Court appointment until 1736.

In 1734 he may have visited Cöthen to inspect the St. Agnus organ, which had been enlarged (B.J. 1925, p. 95); and this year Philipp Emanuel left home to become a student at Frankfurt. This year also, Gesner left Leipzig; and a new Rector, Johann August Ernesti, was installed on Nov. 18.

Ernesti had been Conrector since 1731, and

was at this time on friendly terms with Bach;
he was godfather to Bach's sons Johann August
and Johann Christian on 5 Nov. 1733 and 7
Sept. 1735 respectively. But Ernesti, only 27
when he became Rector, belonged to a later
generation than Bach and Gesner; and he
held the view of his contemporaries, that the
musical obligations of schools such as St.
Thomas' stood in the way of their efficiency
as educational agencies. With on the one hand
a young and tactless man holding such views,
and on the other hand Bach's pugnacious and

TO PAGE 27

obstinate temper, the train was laid; the necessary spark was duly supplied in 1736.

Meanwhile the organist of St. Mary's, Mühlhausen, died on 6 April 1735; Bach wrote two letters to the Council recommending his son Johann Gottfried Bernhard (b. 11 May 1715) for the post. Father and son went to Mühlhausen for the competition, in which Bernhard was successful; he was appointed on June 16 (Mühlhäuser Geschichtsblätter, Jahrg. xxi, 1920-1, p.71). Bach must have felt the departure of his three gifted sons, with whose aid he had in former years been able to 'arrange a concert vocaliter and instrumentaliter' (letter to Erdmann).

In 1736 came the inevitable quarrel with Ernesti. This year one Gottfried Theodor Krause was about to leave the Thomasschule for the University. He was senior prefect; and as such he, like the other prefects, had not only to maintain discipline but also to act as conductor at services and parts of services that were not held to require the presence of the Cantor himself. He had been authorized by Bach to punish offenders, if necessary, on his own account;

TO PAGE 27   163

so on one occasion he caned a boy for bad
conduct at a wedding. The boy said that Krause
had made his back bleed (although the school
hairdresser found 'not the slightest trace' of any
such thing); and complained to Ernesti, who
ordered Krause, a young man of twenty-two,
to be publicly flogged. Ernesti refused to listen
to Krause's pleading, and even to Bach's;
refused to allow Krause to leave the school, and
when he absconded in order to evade what he
claimed to be not punishment but a public
disgrace, impounded his belongings and thirty

thalers held by the school to his credit.

Thus far Krause, in a complaint to the Council dated 26 July 1736. (The above-related events are not dated; but apparently took place in June.) On July 31 the Council ordered that Krause's thirty thalers should be restored to him. And there the matter might have rested, but for Ernesti; who insisted on appointing in Krause's place his namesake Johann Gottlieb Krause, who (it appears) was musically incompetent, and had some time previously been described by Bach, Ernesti not dissenting, as 'a dissolute hound'.

TO PAGE 27

Now the Council's rules for the conduct of the school declared 'it to be the Cantor's prerogative to select as Prefects those scholars whom he regards as fit and competent', and this prerogative had 'been exercised by successive Cantors until now without interference on the part of the Rectors.' So Bach stated his case to the Council on Aug. 12; he had challenged Ernesti on July 10 by sending to him the second prefect (Kittler) with a message that he was to take Krause's place because Bach found the latter incompetent. Krause asked why he had been displaced. He got his answer from Bach; what exactly the latter told him is not known; but he told Ernesti that Bach had degraded him in order to show that the election of prefects was entirely his affair. According to the strict letter of the law Bach should have consulted the Vorsteher of the school; but this he had not done. The Vorsteher was inclined to support Ernesti; and about the middle of July Bach agreed to reinstate Krause. For some reason he did not do so at once; then he was absent from Leipzig until the end of the month; and

TO PAGE 27

when he returned he still did nothing. So on Aug. 11 Ernesti wrote to him to say that unless he acted at once, he would himself reinstate Krause the next morning.

Early next day, Sunday August 12, Bach wrote to the Council the letter from which quotations have been given, asking them 'to instruct Rector Ernesti to act for the future in accordance with the usages and practice of the school.' He then visited Superintendent Deyling to discuss the matter. From Deyling he went on to the church, where he found the service in progress with Krause, reinstated by Ernesti, acting as first prefect. Bach turned him out and put Kittler in his place; informed by Ernesti (who had meanwhile consulted Deyling) that the latter would not support his action, he replied that 'he would not budge an inch from his course, cost what it might.' Ernesti gave orders that Krause and Kittler were to revert to their positions as first and second prefect respectively, and also forbade the choir to sing under any substitute for Krause. Accordingly, at Vespers in St. Nicholas' Bach found Krause

TO PAGE 27

on duty again, and 'chased him from the choir-gallery with much shouting and disturbance.' This time, for fear of Ernesti, Kittler would not take Krause's place; and when he came to supper, Bach 'chased him from the table.'

Next day (Aug. 13) Bach reported Sunday's doings to the Council. Two days later he submitted a report on Krause's character and musical efficiency — or rather, inefficiency; since Bach declared that he 'could not beat even the two ordinary measures [$\frac{4}{4}$ and $\frac{3}{4}$]

accurately.'

Two days later again (Aug. 17) Ernesti sent in his reply: to judge from Terry's summary (the full text is not at hand), that of a man who knows himself to be in the wrong and is reduced to picking holes. He made much of Bach's failure to consult the Vorsteher about the appointment of prefects, and stated (no doubt truthfully) that this was Bach's habit. He claimed that Krause had been satisfactory as third and second prefect, and suggested that the troubles of both the Krauses were in

TO PAGE 27

reality due to the Cantor's absence from his duty.

The Council took no action; and on Sunday Aug. 19 there was again disorder in the churches. That day Bach wrote another letter to the Council, to ask for a quick decision; but they took no notice. Presumably some arrangement was made to prevent further disturbances; but we hear no more of the matter until on Sept. 13 Ernesti wrote to the Council alleging that it was not impossible to bribe Bach ('an old Species thaler made a discantist of one who was no more a discantist than I am'), denying Krause's incompetence, and contradicting Bach on other matters of fact. We are not in a position to check the conflicting statements of Cantor and Rector; but our judgement goes against Ernesti if only because the man who ventured to contradict Bach in matters of elementary musical fact (not taste) must have been a fool.

For five months we hear no more of this affair, for reasons suggested below. In the meantime (from the end of October) Bach's

TO PAGE 27

peace of mind was further troubled by the misdoings of his son Bernhard, who had run up debts at Mühlhausen and now removed thence to Sangerhausen (see note 12, p. 89. Bach's letters to Klemm, now in the Preussische Staatsbibliothek, are printed in Zeitschrift der Sammelbände der Internationalen Musik-Gesellschaft, Jhrg. III (1902), pp. 351-60. Also Mühlhäuser Geschichtsblätter, Jhrg. XXI (1920-1), pp. 78-9). Bernhard passed his tests on 13 Jan. 1737, and was formally appointed on April 4 to the Market Church (also known as St. James').

NOTE 26

PAGE 29

[26] Terry thinks that Bach's appointment at Weissenfels dated from 1729, his honorary Capellmeistership at Cöthen having ended with the death of Prince Leopold. 'Herr Capell Meister Bach' lodged at Weissenfels on 23 Feb. 1729, the Duke's birthday.

The evidence is confusing and contradictory. Walther (p. 70) seems to have thought that Bach became Capellmeister at Weissenfels soon after he went to Leipzig.

When Bach's death was announced in St.

TO PAGE 29 175

Thomas' (31 July 1750) the speaker described him as 'Capellmeister to his Highness of Anhalt-Cöthen'; and the author of the Genealogy says he functioned as honorary Capellmeister to both Weissenfels and Cöthen — this was about 1736. Terry, however, states (p. 265, n. 2) that Bach 'received no appointment at Cöthen' from Leopold's successor.

The matter is of no great importance; but it would be interesting to know exactly how and when Bach was connected with Weissenfels, where there was a good-sized organ with a pedalboard extending to f', a note required for the Toccata in F.

However all this may be Bach's appointment at Weissenfels ended in 1736; the Duke died on June 28, and his Capelle was disbanded. This fact may have some connection with Bach's obtaining, on Nov. 19, the long-coveted post of Court Composer at Dresden. Perhaps Count Kayserling had something to do with it; it was he who paid 100 louis d'or for the Variations named after his employee Goldberg, a harpsichordist who had been a pupil of Bach's in 1733.

TO PAGE 29

At all events, Kayserling received Bach's patent on Nov. 28, and on Dec. 1 Bach gave a recital at the Frauenkirche, Dresden, on a new organ by Silbermann. We do not know whether this recital had been arranged previously, or whether Bach took advantage of having been sent for by Kayserling to receive his patent (Bitter ii, 236; B.J. 1925). The recital referred to as having been given 'some time previously' was perhaps that of 1731 (p. 152).

We now return to the Krause controversy. His attempts to stir the Council to action having failed,

Bach decided to try the Consistorium (the ecclesiastical authority). In November 1736, on or after the 10th, he prepared a letter to them; but did not send it. Presumably the news of his Court appointment led him to hope for Electoral assistance. In this he was disappointed; and on 12 Feb. 1737 he redated the November letter (which is why the original date is uncertain) and despatched it. Next day the Consistorium asked the Council to attend to Bach's complaint without delay. But Krause was leaving the school at Easter (Ap. 21); and the Council thought this

TO PAGE 29

a heaven-sent opportunity of letting the matter drop. They had, as a matter of fact, already decided on Feb. 6 that Bach's claim to appoint prefects was lawful; but they hesitated to condemn Ernesti, and kept their decision secret until April, when it was communicated to Ernesti on the 6th, Bach on the 10th, and Superintendent Deyling on the 20th. No further action was taken until Aug. 21, when Bach wrote again to the Consistorium. Still he failed to obtain satisfaction; so on Oct. 18 he appealed to the Elector, who now at last took action. On Dec. 17 a document was prepared demanding that Bach's complaints should receive consideration. This was before the Consistorium on 1 Feb. 1738 and the Council on Feb. 5. We hear no more of the matter. Some compromise must have been made; perhaps at the end of April, when the Elector had occasion to visit Leipzig (27th), and heard, at a University function, an adulatory cantata with music by Bach — not by Görner. The old controversy was revived, but settled in Bach's favour by (one supposes) the University students, who paid.

TO PAGE 29

For the rest of his life Bach does not seem to have been seriously interfered with by his employers.

The school controversy was not Bach's only trouble during 1737. Johann Adolf Scheibe, son of Johann Scheibe who built the organs in St. Paul's and St. John's, Leipzig, had applied for the organistship of St. Thomas' in 1729. Görner was appointed; and Scheibe made no secret of his thinking that he had a grievance against Bach, who had been one of the judges. On 5 Mar. 1737 he started a periodical 'Der critische Musicus' at Hamburg, in which (May 14) he made an attack on Bach as a composer. J. A. Birnbaum replied in a pamphlet published in Jan. 1738, and the controversy dragged on into the following year.

For the years 1738 to 1742 we have a few intimate details of Bach's home life, thanks to the letters of his cousin Johann Elias Bach (Die Musik, 1912-13, pp. 3-19). Elias, thirty-three years old in 1738, was a divinity student at Leipzig University, and acted as tutor to the three surviving sons of Bach's second marriage.

TO PAGE 29

In the spring of 1738 Bernhard Bach absconded from Sangerhausen, where, as at Mühlhausen, he had got into debt. This affair is the subject of Bach's letters of May 24 and 26 to the Klemms. Bernhard, whose whereabouts were unknown to his father even as late as October, matriculated at Jena on 28 Jan. 1739, and died there of fever on May 27.

It is from Elias' letters of 10 Jan. and 28 Sept. 1739 that we learn of the publication of the Clavierübung, Part III, between those dates.

NOTE 26

In July 1739 Friedemann visited his father for a month's holiday, bringing with him two celebrated lutanists. Bach's compositions for the lute were probably inspired by this visit; and a few months later he kept up the family tradition (p.3) by inventing the 'Lautenclavicymbel', a combination of lute and harpsichord. A specimen instrument was built for him by Zacharias Hildebrand.

About this time Prince Augustus Ludwig of Cöthen visited Leipzig for a cure, and Bach took part in a celebration of his birthday on

TO PAGE 29 185

Aug. 3. He also produced a cantata for the Elector's birthday on Oct. 7 (1739). He was still conductor of the Collegium Musicum, an orchestral society made up of University students, with which he had been connected since 1729; but he had practically ceased to compose for the church, and was about to withdraw himself almost completely from public music-making in Leipzig. In the last ten years of his life he was frequently out of Leipzig on various errands; and at home he concentrated on organ and clavier music, in particular on preparing some few works for engraving and publication.

In 1741 Emanuel became accompanist to Frederick the Great, and Bach visited him in Berlin although Prussia was at war. He should have gone in June; but his visit was postponed until July, and was probably shortened by an illness of Anna Magdalena's, of which he learnt from letters of Elias' dated Aug. 5 and 9. In November he and Elias visited Kayserling at Dresden. In 1742 the Goldberg Variations were published.

In 1744 Bach examined the organ at St.

TO PAGE 29

Paul's, Leipzig, built by Johann Scheibe, the father of Johann Adolph Scheibe who had attacked Bach in 1737. The same year he completed the Second Part of the 'Forty-Eight' (defective autograph in the British Museum, Add. MS. 35021). In 1746 (Aug. 7) he examined an organ at Zschortau (certificate in the British Museum, Add. MS. 33965, fol. 168); and on Sept. 27 he and Silbermann tested an organ by Zacharias Hildebrand at St. Wenceslas', Naumburg — the church to which Altnikol became organist, on Bach's recommendation, in 1748.

PAGE 30

[27] Emanuel had married in 1744; a son was born to him on 30 Nov. 1745. This was the first marriage in Bach's family; but it does not appear that he visited Emanuel between 1741 and the spring of 1747. On this latter occasion he took Friedemann with him. The latter was probably the source for Forkel's account of the visit to Frederick the Great; which is no reason for regarding that account as strictly trustworthy.

TO PAGE 30

Most probably Frederick heard of Bach's presence in Berlin from Emanuel. He seems to have sent for Bach, who arrived in Potsdam on the evening of Sunday May 7; the King was just preparing for his usual evening concert. Bach was announced; the King exclaimed, 'Gentlemen, Old Bach is here,' abandoned with his concert the more than military regularity of his habits, and spent the evening listening to Bach. The word 'pianoforte' is to be observed; Frederick had a number of the early Silbermann instruments.

NOTE 27

On May 8 Bach gave an organ recital in the garrison church, Potsdam. According to one account it was this day that he extemporized the six-part fugue — the truth, as with the Marchand affair, is probably hopelessly buried beneath the inventions of Bach's sons. He returned to Berlin, and there inspected the new Opera House, astonishing his companions by deducing from the shape of the 'grand saloon' that it would give a whispering-gallery effect.

In June 1747 he joined Mizler's Society for the Promotion of Musical Science (p. 214).

TO PAGE 30   191

In 1748 Elias (since 29 May 1743 Cantor at Schweinfurt) asked Bach for a copy of 'the Prussian fuge' (some part of the Musicalische Opfer, but which I cannot say at present). Bach replied on Oct. 6: 'justement to-day the edition is sold out. Only 100 copies were engraved, and most of them I gave away gratis to friends. However, between now and New Year's Fair more will be published, and if my cousin still desires an exemplar he should acquaint me with an opportunity to dispatch it, send me a thaler post, and it will be forwarded.'

NOTE 27

Elias sent a cask of wine with his reply; and on Nov. 2 Bach acknowledged the gift. Here is his letter in full:

Worthy and respected cousin,
 Your letter, received yesterday, brings me the good news that you and your dear wife are well, and for the delectable cask of wine that came with it accept my best thanks. Unfortunately the cask suffered a jar, or some other accident, on the journey, for on examination here it is found to be one-third empty and

TO PAGE 30

contains, the Visitator declares, only six Kannen. It is regrettable that the smallest drop of so noble a gift of God should be wasted, but I am none the less heartily obliged by my worthy cousin's kind present. Pro nunc I am not reellement in a position to reciprocate; still, quod differtur non auffertur, and I hope to find an opportunity to discharge my obligation.

It is unfortunate that we live so far apart, for else I should give myself the pleasure of inviting her cousin to my daughter Lissgen's wedding, which takes place in January 1749,

NOTE 27

to the new Naumburg organist Herr Altnikol. However, though for that reason, and because of the inconvenient season, he cannot be present, I will ask him to assist them with his good wishes, and with the same I commend myself to my good cousin's remembrance. With warmest greetings to you from all here, I remain

    Your Honour's devoted and faithful cousin + servant to command,

    Joh. Seb. Bach.

Leipzig, 2 November 1748.

P.S. Magister Birnbaum was buried six

TO PAGE 30

weeks ago.

P.M. Though my good cousin offers to send me more of the same <u>liqueur</u>, I must decline on account of the heavy charges at this end. The carriage was 16 gr., delivery 2 gr., <u>Visitator</u> 2 gr., provincial excise 5 gr. 3 pfg., general excise 3 gr. So my cousin may calculate that the wine cost me nearly 5 gr. a measure, a too expensive present!

A Monsieur J. E. Bach, Chanteur [Cantor] et Inspecteur des Gymnasiastes de la Ville Imperialle à Schweinfourth, Franqué Coburg.

Lissgen (Elisabeth Juliane Friederica Bach) married Johann Christoph Altnikol, who had been a pupil of Bach's (see also p. 187), on 20 Jan. 1749.

In the early summer of 1749 Bach was evidently ill; Terry thinks, apparently on the evidence of Taylor the 'eye-doctor', that he had a stroke about May. In June one Harrer was tested with a view to his being appointed in Bach's place; but the latter recovered.

On 12 May 1749 one Biedermann, Rector of the Freiberg Gymnasium, saw fit to denounce

TO PAGE 30

the study of music on the grounds that it was bad for the morals: he chose Caligula and Nero as examples. A controversy broke out; one Schröter, a member of Mizler's Society, wrote a reply, apparently at Bach's request; this was approved by Bach and published in 1750 (Bitter iii, 236). Schröter then found that his text had been altered, and accused Bach. The latter wrote on May 26 to an intermediary to say that he could not at present write to Schröter, but was not to blame for the alterations.

NOTE 28

PAGE 32

[28] The above-mentioned letter to Schröter was probably dictated, not written by Bach himself; though this is not known for certain. It is unlikely, however, that by May 1750 Bach's sight would have allowed him to write.

The 'eye-doctor' whom he consulted, perhaps
? at the end of 1749, was the Chevalier John Taylor, an English charlatan. According to Terry, Taylor was again in Leipzig in Jan. 1750, on his way from Vienna to Mecklenburg. Ilse Hecht (Musical Times, March 1938, p.175) shows that he

see M & L April 1938

TO PAGE 32

was lecturing in Leipzig on Mar. 28. It happens that Bach's ability to write at this time has some bearing on the text of the 'Vom Himmel hoch' Variations; and it is unfortunate that we cannot date his operations.

It has been held that the autograph text of the Variations dates from 1750, and is therefore later than that of the engraved edition, which apparently was published about 1747. I believe that this theory — and with it the idea that the Autograph text is superior — is conclusively disproved by a correction in the last bars of the Canon by Augmentation; but it would be useful to know for certain that Bach was incapable of writing after Jan. 1750.

Whether the following famous story has some early authority, or is simply a (legitimate) deduction from the state of the MS., I do not know.

In his last days Bach dictated to Altnikol an expanded and drastically revised version of the Orgelbüchlein prelude 'Wenn wir in höchsten Nöthen sein' (When we are in deepest need). But Bach was not now thinking of that

TO PAGE 32

hymn; he had in his mind one even more appropriate to his condition:

> Before Thy throne, my God, I stand,
> Myself, my all, are in Thy hand;
> . . . .
>
> Grant that my end may worthy be,
> And that I wake Thy face to see,
> Thyself for evermore to know!
> Amen, Amen, God grant it so!
>   (tr. C. S. Terry)

and he had the prelude headed accordingly, 'Vor deinen Thron tret ich hiemit'. It is very generally overrated, on account of its sentimental interest. For some reason only part of it appears in the MS.; the complete work was published with the Art of Fugue, apparently to compensate for the incompleteness of that work.

Bach was buried on 31 July 1750 near the south wall of St. John's Church. On the 29th the Council had already met to consider the appointment of Harrer in his place; they had the grace to defer their decision until Aug. 7. On this 29th they had referred to Bach as 'the Cantor of St. Thomas' School, or rather Capell-

TO PAGE 32

Director Bach'; and one of them said, 'The School needs a Cantor not a Capellmeister; although certainly he ought to understand music.' These words were uttered by one Stieglitz. It is well that the name of this typical Councillor should be remembered.

The exact site of Bach's grave was soon forgotten; but in 1894 opportunity occurred to make excavations, and on Oct. 22 there was unearthed what has been accepted as Bach's skeleton. The remains were placed beneath the altar of the church.

PAGE 35

[29] The Clavierübung, Part I, consists of the six Partitas; these were published singly, one each year from 1726 onwards (p. 138), and then all together in 1731. According to Forkel, they were in some demand.

The original edition of the Nekrolog has 'pages' (Seiten) for 'suites' (Suiten).

Part II, the Italian Concerto and Overture in B minor (Overture here means Suite: the work is that which includes the 'Echo' movement), appeared in 1735; Part III (the Catechism Preludes)

TO PAGE 35

in 1739; and the 'Aria with Thirty Variations', Part IV, in 1742.

The Six Preludes, known as the 'Schüblers' from the publisher's name, probably appeared in 1746. Five of them are arrangements of vocal movements from the Cantatas, and the sixth is presumably a similar arrangement from a lost Cantata.

The Canonic Variations probably appeared about 1747. The dedicatory letter of the Musical Offering is dated 7 July 1747 (I think only part of the work was engraved at this date). The

Art of Fugue, partly engraved before Bach's death, was published, I think, in 1751; there was a second edition.

PAGE 38

3° The following identifications and remarks may be useful:

2 'Masses' — includes the short Lutheran Masses as well as the B minor. 'Oratorios' — only the Christmas Oratorio is well known under that title; but Cantata 11 is also known as the Ascension Oratorio, and I believe there is an Easter one. The Magnificat referred to

TO PAGES 35-38   207

is that in D, not Cantata 10.

   3 Five Passions. Emanuel may have included the St. Luke Passion, now rejected as spurious. Only two genuine Passions are now known.

   4 Not all the Motets are for double choir.

   6 These are the Sonatas.

   8 Probably the Orgelbüchlein.

   9 The Forty-Eight: Part I 1722, Part II 1744.

  11 The 'English' Suites.

  12 The 'French' Suites.

  13 'without bass'; i.e., without figured bass,

unaccompanied.

In an undated letter to Forkel (Bach-Urkunden) Emanuel adds to this list the Inventions and Six Short Preludes (all for clavier). His catalogue seems to consist chiefly of works in his own possession. We have a fair idea of the MSS. that came into his hands, from a list of (MS.) music that his widow published — the MSS. were for sale. The British Museum has a copy of this list.

PAGE 39

3¹ Maria Barbara Bach was born 20 Oct.

1684, married Sebastian at Dornheim 17 Oct. 1707, and was buried 4 July 1720.

[32] Wilhelm Friedemann Bach was born 22 Nov. 1710; began his musical education 22 Jan. 1720, with the Clavierbüchlein; became organist of St. Sophia's, Dresden, in 1733 (p. 155); moved to Halle in 1746; later resigned that post, took to drink, and finally died in poverty 1 July 1784.

Carl Philipp Emanuel Bach was born 8 Mar. 1714; became a student at Frankfurt

1734; accompanist to Frederick the Great 1741; Capellmeister at Hamburg, 1767; died 15 Dec. 1788.

PAGE 40

33 Anna Magdalena Wilcken (the name is spelt in several different ways) was baptized 22 Sept. 1701. She was a singer ('a very clear soprano' says Bach in his letter to Erdmann) and was employed as such at the court of Anhalt-Zerbst, and then from the autumn of 1720 at Cöthen. She had been to Cöthen as a visitor before that time. She retained her pos-

ition as a soprano after her marriage, which took place on 3 Dec. 1721. Bach made two music-books for her, the Clavierbüchlein in 1722 and the Notenbuch in 1725.

PAGE 41

34 Gottfried Heinrich (d. 1763) was half-witted. Elisabeth's marriage has been referred to (pp. 193, 196); Altnikol died in 1759. Johann Christoph, born 21 June 1732, took up his position as Chamber Musician early in 1750, and became known as the Bückeburg Bach. He died 26 Jan. 1795. Johann Christian, born 5 Sept. 1735, studied in

Italy, became an opera composer, and died in London 1 Jan. 1782. Johanna Carolina died in 1781; Regina Susanna survived until 1809.

Anna Magdalena's own children were in 1750 too young to be able to support her; and her step-children, to their lasting disgrace, took no pains to do so. She lived on as an alms-woman, and on 27 Feb. 1760 received a pauper's funeral.

PAGE 48

35 The organ referred to was that in St. John's, Leipzig; for the 'certain circumstances' see

TO PAGES 41-49   213

pp. 186, 181.

PAGE 49

36 'schönen und nie gehörten Erfindungen im Orgelspielen'. I do not understand this.

37 Bach was also a string-player. In private music-makings he played the viola, because it placed him in the middle of the harmony. His compositions show that he had a thorough knowledge of string technique.

He is also said to have practised music-engraving; and certainly parts of the Clavierübung, Part III, are engraved in a 'hand' very similar to Bach's.

PAGE 50

[38] Here begins Mizler's contribution to the Nekrolog.

Lorentz Christoph Mizler graduated at Leipzig in 1734. In 1736 he started the 'Neu eröffnete musicalische Bibliothek', and in 1738 founded his Society. The members were men who held some sort of musical position and were not merely executants. They did not meet, but circulated music and articles among

TO PAGES 49-50

themselves and contributed theoretical papers to the Musicalischer Bibliothek. The Society had a library, on whose walls were hung portraits of the members; these they had to present when they were elected.

Bach's portrait was the work of the Dresden Court painter E.G. Haussmann. When the Society broke up, the portrait went to the Thomasschule; it is now in the old Rathaus. It shows Bach holding in his hand the canon referred to in the text. This is the most familiar portrait; but one suspects that it is far less characteristic than that which was discovered by Fritz Volbach in 1904 (*Die Musik*, Jahrg. IX, Okt.-Dez. 1909, p. 107; reproductions in Schweitzer and Parry).

Emanuel's opinion of the Society's 'deep theoretical speculations' is made indecently clear by his remarks quoted on p. xiv.

It is supposed that Bach's diploma piece was the Canonic Variations. Unfortunately, the date of publication of the engraved text cannot be closely determined, which makes matters no easier for the editor, whose first business is to find out whether the engraved or the autograph

TO PAGE 50

text is the later. My own view is that when Bach had made his usual rough draft of the work, he fair-copied it twice: one copy (lost) was for circulation in the Society, and was itself copied: the other, for his own use, he made in the MS. that already contained the Organ Sonatas and some of (what we call) the Eighteen Chorale-Preludes. Later he decided to engrave the work, and revised it for that purpose.

Mizler's words (p.51) are important. It will be seen that he distinguishes between the 'completely worked out' version presented to the Society and that which was engraved 'afterwards'. The meaning of the words 'completely worked out' is clear enough: the copy supplied to the Society was written out in full, whereas in the engraved edition the answering parts of the canons are omitted (perhaps to save expense). The missing parts, being (almost) exact transpositions of the leaders, could easily be supplied by anyone who wished to make himself a copy to play from.

PAGE 51

39 Cf. Bitter iii, 211. It is a triple Canon in six

TO PAGES 50, 51, & 67   219

parts — whatever that may mean. In the portrait and the Nekrolog it appears in puzzle-canon form; a full working-out is in C.L. Hilgenfeldt, Johann Sebastian Bachs Leben, Wirken und Werke, Leipzig 1850, Table 3.

The text given here (p. [63]) is copied from Terry. I have not had access either to the original edition of the Nekrolog or even to the B.G.

PAGE [67]

4° Johann Gottfried Walther (1684–1748) was organist of the Town Church at Weimar from 1707 until his death. He was a composer of some ability, his speciality being organ chorale-preludes; and his Musical Dictionary is an important work of reference.

Walther and Bach were distantly and obscurely related through the Lämmerhirt family, and were intimate, it seems, while Bach was in Weimar. Bach stood godfather to Walther's eldest son on 26 Sept. 1712. Forkel has an anecdote of their friendly rivalry at the clavier.

From the brevity and tone of Walther's article Spitta deduced that he and Bach must have become estranged; but the evidence seems in-

TO PAGES 67-71

sufficient, and in any case the matter is of no particular importance.

PAGE 69

4¹ The date is correct.

4² The word 'came' and on p. 70 'here' show how an author may give away information about himself quite unconsciously. Cf. preface to the Saga of the Ere-dwellers, Saga Library II.

PAGE 70

43 See p. 174.

PAGE 71

44 See p. 204.

45 Perhaps Walther got this idea from Bach himself. See p. 81.

46 H is, of course, b natural; and b is b flat. The ticks indicate pitch — b' is middle b flat on the piano keyboard.

The clavier Prelude and Fugue on BACH is of doubtful authenticity; Bach seems to have used his own name only once: as the third subject of the unfinished Contrapunctus in the Art of Fugue.

PAGE [73]

47 The translation is taken from the facsimile

TO PAGES 71–73   223

in Bach-Urkunden; that is to say, from the copy of the Genealogy that belonged to Emanuel and was partly brought up to date by him before he handed it over to Forkel.

The great puzzle about the Genealogy is that on the one hand the phrase 'according to God's holy Will' leaves us in little doubt that the wording is Sebastian's; but if this is so, we have to account for his giving a wrong date for his own first organ appointment, and not knowing where or when his eldest brother was born, or when he died.

The Genealogy contains 53 entries dealing with male Bachs from Veit to Sebastian's children. It must have been compiled about 1736, since it records the birth of Johann Christian (5 Sept. 1735), but not Sebastian's appointment as Court Composer (19 Nov. 1736).

The passage in { } is an insertion by Emanuel, made presumably in 1774 or 5, when he handed the MS. over to Forkel. It will be observed that he gives a wrong date for Bach's death.

PAGE 75

48 So the MS. Read 1703. Cf. p. 94.
49 See p. 101.

PAGE 76

50 See p. 174.
51 Read 28 July.

POSTSCRIPT

ANYONE who has read the Dedicatory Note and Introduction will see that this book has been meant to be divers things at sundry times; and now is perhaps something quite different again. The fact is, it has been put together in bits and pieces. The preliminary matter was written after the translation, but long before the notes were finished; and fair-copying and annotation went on together. Hence

228　　　　　　　　POSTSCRIPT

certain inconsistencies.

　Now that the job is done I can describe the scope of the Notes more accurately. They are a summary of Terry's Biography — i.e. of the latest modern research. A few incidents, unlikely to be of importance to me and of no special interest to anyone, I have left altogether unmentioned. I am afraid I have included an exasperating number of mere dates; but they are the editor's bread and butter, and I only wish we had more of them.

　Glancing over the whole to remove the grosser

POSTSCRIPT

errors, I have found one or two points that need comment. There are probably others.

On p. xvii read Musicalisches (for Musik-).

On p. 12, line 7, 'indirectly' would be better than 'incidentally'.

Page 15, line 1: 'In 1703 he came to Weimar.' See note 42, p. 221. On this principle Emanuel or Agricola (or both) wrote this passage at Weimar. But I doubt it. Probably they regarded Bach's move to Weimar as a return (to Thuringia from far-off Lüneburg), and for that reason used the word 'came'. A warning, perhaps, to textual critics; like Knox's Essays in Satire; though of course I might find, if I were in a position to make the necessary investigations, that Agricola held a post at Weimar at some time or other. Emanuel certainly did not.

Page 32: 'a quarter to nine'; so Terry. I suppose he knew what 'nach einem Viertel auf 9 Uhr' means; I don't.

Pages 34 and 37. I suppose there is some significance in the use of 'vor' instead of 'über'; but I don't know what it is.

POSTSCRIPT

Page 181. For Adolf read Adolph. (That Man again!)

BEGUN AT BEDFORD in October 1941; continued at Market Warsop, and finished 19 Jan. 1942.

Walter Emery

Music and Books published by Travis & Emery Music Bookshop:

Anon.: Hymnarium Sarisburiense, cum Rubricis et Notis Musicis.
Agricola, Johann Friedrich from Tosi: Anleitung zur Singkunst.
Bach, C.P.E.: edited W. Emery: Nekrolog or Obituary Notice of J.S. Bach.
Bateson, Naomi Judith: Alcock of Salisbury
Bathe, William: A Briefe Introduction to the Skill of Song
Bax, Arnold: Symphony #5, Arranged for Piano Four Hands by Walter Emery
Burney, Charles: The Present State of Music in France and Italy
Burney, Charles: The Present State of Music in Germany, The Netherlands ...
Burney, Charles: An Account of the Musical Performances ... Handel
Burney, Karl: Nachricht von Georg Friedrich Handel's Lebensumstanden.
Burns, Robert: The Caledonian Musical Museum ..The Best Scotch Songs. (1810)
Cobbett, W.W.: Cobbett's Cyclopedic Survey of Chamber Music. (2 vols.)
Corrette, Michel: Le Maitre de Clavecin
Crimp, Bryan: Dear Mr. Rosenthal ... Dear Mr. Gaisberg ...
Crimp, Bryan: Solo: The Biography of Solomon
d'Indy, Vincent: Beethoven: Biographie Critique
d'Indy, Vincent: Beethoven: A Critical Biography
d'Indy, Vincent: César Franck (in French)
Fischhof, Joseph: Versuch einer Geschichte des Clavierbaues. (Faksimile 1853).
Frescobaldi, Girolamo: D'Arie Musicali per Cantarsi. Primo & Secondo Libro.
Geminiani, Francesco: The Art of Playing the Violin.
Handel; Purcell; Boyce; Geene et al: Calliope or English Harmony: Volume First.
Häuser: Musikalisches Lexikon. 2 vols in one.
Hawkins, John: A General History of the Science and Practice of Music (5 vols.)
Herbert-Caesari, Edgar: The Science and Sensations of Vocal Tone
Herbert-Caesari, Edgar: Vocal Truth
Hopkins and Rimboult: The Organ. Its History and Construction.
Hunt, John: - see separate list of discographies at the end of these titles
Isaacs, Lewis: Hänsel and Gretel. A Guide to Humperdinck's Opera.
Isaacs, Lewis: Königskinder (Royal Children) A Guide to Humperdinck's Opera.
Kastner: Manuel Général de Musique Militaire
Lacassagne, M. l'Abbé Joseph : Traité Général des élémens du Chant.
Lascelles (née Catley), Anne: The Life of Miss Anne Catley.
Mainwaring, John: Memoirs of the Life of the Late George Frederic Handel
Malcolm, Alexander: A Treaty of Music: Speculative, Practical and Historical
Marx, Adolph Bernhard: Die Kunst des Gesanges, Theoretisch-Practisch
May, Florence: The Life of Brahms
May, Florence: The Girlhood Of Clara Schumann: Clara Wieck And Her Time.
Mellers, Wilfrid: Angels of the Night: Popular Female Singers of Our Time
Mellers, Wilfrid: Bach and the Dance of God
Mellers, Wilfrid: Beethoven and the Voice of God
Mellers, Wilfrid: Caliban Reborn - Renewal in Twentieth Century Music

Music and Books published by Travis & Emery Music Bookshop:
Mellers, Wilfrid: Darker Shade of Pale, A Backdrop to Bob Dylan
Mellers, Wilfrid: François Couperin and the French Classical Tradition
Mellers, Wilfrid: Harmonious Meeting
Mellers, Wilfrid: Le Jardin Retrouvé, The Music of Frederic Mompou
Mellers, Wilfrid: Music and Society, England and the European Tradition
Mellers, Wilfrid: Music in a New Found Land: ...... American Music
Mellers, Wilfrid: Romanticism and the Twentieth Century (from 1800)
Mellers, Wilfrid: The Masks of Orpheus: ...... the Story of European Music.
Mellers, Wilfrid: The Sonata Principle (from c. 1750)
Mellers, Wilfrid: Vaughan Williams and the Vision of Albion
Panchianio, Cattuffio: Rutzvanscad Il Giovine
Pearce, Charles: Sims Reeves, Fifty Years of Music in England.
Playford, John: An Introduction to the Skill of Musick.
Purcell, Henry et al: Harmonia Sacra ... The First Book, (1726)
Purcell, Henry et al: Harmonia Sacra ... Book II (1726)
Quantz, Johann: Versuch einer Anweisung die Flöte trave rsiere zu spielen.
Rameau, Jean-Philippe: Code de Musique Pratique, ou Methodes.
Rastall, Richard: The Notation of Western Music.
Rimbault, Edward: The Pianoforte, Its Origins, Progress, and Construction.
Rousseau, Jean Jacques: Dictionnaire de Musique
Rubinstein, Anton : Guide to the proper use of the Pianoforte Pedals.
Sainsbury, John S.: Dictionary of Musicians. (1825). 2 vols.
Serré de Rieux, Jean de : Les dons des Enfans de Latone
Simpson, Christopher: A Compendium of Practical Musick in Five Parts
Spohr, Louis: Autobiography
Spohr, Louis: Grand Violin School
Tans'ur, William: A New Musical Grammar; or The Harmonical Spectator
Terry, Charles Sanford: Bach's Chorals – Parts 1, 2 and 3.
Terry, Charles Sanford: John Christian Bach
Terry, Charles Sanford: J.S. Bach's Original Hymn-Tunes for Congregational Use.
Terry, Charles Sanford: Four-Part Chorals of J.S. Bach. (German & English)
Terry, Charles Sanford: Joh. Seb. Bach, Cantata Texts, Sacred and Secular.
Terry, Charles Sanford: The Origins of the Family of Bach Musicians.
Tosi, Pierfrancesco: Opinioni de' Cantori Antichi, e Moderni
Tosi, Pierfrancesco: Observations on the Florid Song.
Van der Straeten, Edmund: History of the Violoncello, The Viol da Gamba ...
Van der Straeten, Edmund: History of the Violin, Its Ancestors... (2 vols.)
Walther, J. G. [Waltern]: Musicalisches Lexikon [Musikalisches Lexicon]
Zwirn, Gerald: Stranded Stories From The Operas

Travis & Emery Music Bookshop
17 Cecil Court, London, WC2N 4EZ, United Kingdom.
Tel. (+44) 20 7240 2129

© Travis & Emery 2010

Discographies by Travis & Emery:
Discographies by John Hunt.

1987: 978-1-906857-14-1: From Adam to Webern: the Recordings of von Karajan.
1991: 978-0-951026-83-0: 3 Italian Conductors and 7 Viennese Sopranos: 10 Discographies: Arturo Toscanini, Guido Cantelli, Carlo Maria Giulini, Elisabeth Schwarzkopf, Irmgard Seefried, Elisabeth Gruemmer, Sena Jurinac, Hilde Gueden, Lisa Della Casa, Rita Streich.
1992: 978-0-951026-85-4: Mid-Century Conductors and More Viennese Singers: 10 Discographies: Karl Boehm, Victor De Sabata, Hans Knappertsbusch, Tullio Serafin, Clemens Krauss, Anton Dermota, Leonie Rysanek, Eberhard Waechter, Maria Reining, Erich Kunz.
1993: 978-0-951026-87-8: More 20th Century Conductors: 7 Discographies: Eugen Jochum, Ferenc Fricsay, Carl Schuricht, Felix Weingartner, Josef Krips, Otto Klemperer, Erich Kleiber.
1994: 978-0-951026-88-5: Giants of the Keyboard: 6 Discographies: Wilhelm Kempff, Walter Gieseking, Edwin Fischer, Clara Haskil, Wilhelm Backhaus, Artur Schnabel.
1994: 978-0-951026-89-2: Six Wagnerian Sopranos: 6 Discographies: Frieda Leider, Kirsten Flagstad, Astrid Varnay, Martha Moedl, Birgit Nilsson, Gwyneth Jones.
1995: 978-0-952582-70-0: Musical Knights: 6 Discographies: Henry Wood, Thomas Beecham, Adrian Boult, John Barbirolli, Reginald Goodall, Malcolm Sargent.
1995: 978-0-952582-71-7: A Notable Quartet: 4 Discographies: Gundula Janowitz, Christa Ludwig, Nicolai Gedda, Dietrich Fischer-Dieskau.
1996: 978-0-952582-75-5: Leopold Stokowski (1882-1977): Discography and Concert Register
1996: 978-0-952582-76-2: Makers of the Philharmonia: 11 Discographies: Alceo Galliera, Walter Susskind, Paul Kletzki, Nicolai Malko, Issay Dobrowen, Lovro Von Matacic, Efrem Kurtz, Otto Ackermann, Anatole Fistoulari, George Weldon, Robert Irving.
1996: 978-0-952582-72-4: The Post-War German Tradition: 5 Discographies: Rudolf Kempe, Joseph Keilberth, Wolfgang Sawallisch, Rafael Kubelik, Andre Cluytens.
1996: 978-0-952582-73-1: Teachers and Pupils: 7 Discographies: Elisabeth Schwarzkopf, Maria Ivoguen, Maria Cebotari, Meta Seinemeyer, Ljuba Welitsch, Rita Streich, Erna Berger.
1996: 978-0-952582-75-5: Leopold Stokowski: Discography and Concert Listing.
1996: 978-0-952582-76-2: Makers of the Philharmonia: 11 Discographies Alceo Galliera, Walter Susskind, Paul Kletzki, Nicolai Malko, Issay Dobrowen, Lovro Von Matacic, Efrem Kurtz, Otto Ackermann, Anatole Fistoulari, George Weldon, Robert Irving.
1996: 978-0-952582-77-9: Tenors in a Lyric Tradition: 3 Discographies: Peter Anders, Walther Ludwig, Fritz Wunderlich.
1997: 978-0-952582-78-6: The Lyric Baritone: 5 Discographies: Hans Reinmar, Gerhard Huesch, Josef Metternich, Hermann Uhde, Eberhard Waechter.
1997: 978-0-952582-79-3: Hungarians in Exile: 3 Discographies: Fritz Reiner, Antal Dorati, George Szell.
1997: 978-1-901395-00-6: The Art of the Diva: 3 Discographies: Claudia Muzio, Maria Callas, Magda Olivero.
1997: 978-1-901395-01-3: Metropolitan Sopranos: 4 Discographies: Rosa Ponselle, Eleanor Steber, Zinka Milanov, Leontyne Price.
1997: 978-1-901395-02-0: Back From The Shadows: 4 Discographies: Willem Mengelberg, Dimitri Mitropoulos, Hermann Abendroth, Eduard Van Beinum.
1997: 978-1-901395-03-7: More Musical Knights: 4 Discographies: Hamilton Harty, Charles Mackerras, Simon Rattle, John Pritchard.
1998: 978-1-901395-95-2: More Giants of the Keyboard: 5 Discographies: Claudio Arrau, Gyorgy Cziffra, Vladimir Horowitz, Dinu Lipatti, Artur Rubinstein.

1998: 978-1-901395-94-5: Conductors On The Yellow Label: 8 Discographies: Fritz Lehmann, Ferdinand Leitner, Ferenc Fricsay, Eugen Jochum, Leopold Ludwig, Artur Rother, Franz Konwitschny, Igor Markevitch.
1998: 978-1-901395-96-9: Mezzo and Contraltos: 5 Discographies: Janet Baker, Margarete Klose, Kathleen Ferrier, Giulietta Simionato, Elisabeth Hoengen.
1999: 978-1-901395-97-6: The Furtwaengler Sound Sixth Edition: Discography and Concert Listing.
1999: 978-1-901395-98-3: The Great Dictators: 3 Discographies: Evgeny Mravinsky, Artur Rodzinski, Sergiu Celibidache.
1999: 978-1-901395-99-0: Sviatoslav Richter: Pianist of the Century: Discography.
2000: 978-1-901395-04-4: Philharmonic Autocrat 1: Discography of: Herbert Von Karajan [Third Edition].
2000: 978-1-901395-05-1: Wiener Philharmoniker 1 - Vienna Philharmonic and Vienna State Opera Orchestras: Discography Part 1 1905-1954.
2000: 978-1-901395-06-8: Wiener Philharmoniker 2 - Vienna Philharmonic and Vienna State Opera Orchestras: Discography Part 2 1954-1989.
2001: 978-1-901395-07-5: Gramophone Stalwarts: 3 Separate Discographies: Bruno Walter, Erich Leinsdorf, Georg Solti.
2001: 978-1-901395-08-2: Singers of the Third Reich: 5 Discographies: Helge Roswaenge, Tiana Lemnitz, Franz Voelker, Maria Mueller, Max Lorenz.
2001: 978-1-901395-09-9: Philharmonic Autocrat 2: Concert Register of Herbert Von Karajan Second Edition.
2002: 978-1-901395-10-5: Sächsische Staatskapelle Dresden: Complete Discography.
2002: 978-1-901395-11-2: Carlo Maria Giulini: Discography and Concert Register.
2002: 978-1-901395-12-9: Pianists For The Connoisseur: 6 Discographies: Arturo Benedetti Michelangeli, Alfred Cortot, Alexis Weissenberg, Clifford Curzon, Solomon, Elly Ney.
2003: 978-1-901395-14-3: Singers on the Yellow Label: 7 Discographies: Maria Stader, Elfriede Troetschel, Annelies Kupper, Wolfgang Windgassen, Ernst Haefliger, Josef Greindl, Kim Borg.
2003: 978-1-901395-15-0: A Gallic Trio: 3 Discographies: Charles Muench, Paul Paray, Pierre Monteux.
2004: 978-1-901395-16-7: Antal Dorati 1906-1988: Discography and Concert Register.
2004: 978-1-901395-17-4: Columbia 33CX Label Discography.
2004: 978-1-901395-18-1: Great Violinists: 3 Discographies: David Oistrakh, Wolfgang Schneiderhan, Arthur Grumiaux.
2006: 978-1-901395-19-8: Leopold Stokowski: Second Edition of the Discography.
2006: 978-1-901395-20-4: Wagner Im Festspielhaus: Discography of the Bayreuth Festival.
2006: 978-1-901395-21-1: Her Master's Voice: Concert Register and Discography of Dame Elisabeth Schwarzkopf [Third Edition].
2007: 978-1-901395-22-8: Hans Knappertsbusch: Kna: Concert Register and Discography of Hans Knappertsbusch, 1888-1965. Second Edition.
2008: 978-1-901395-23-5: Philips Minigroove: Second Extended Version of the European Discography.
2009: 978-1-901395-24-2: American Classics: The Discographies of Leonard Bernstein and Eugene Ormandy.
2010: 978-1-901395-25-9: Dirigenten der DDR: Conductors of the German Democratic Republic

Discography by Stephen J. Pettitt, edited by John Hunt:
1987: 978-1-906857-16-5: Philharmonia Orchestra: Complete Discography 1945-1987

Available from: Travis & Emery at 17 Cecil Court, London, UK. (+44) 20 7 240 2129. email on sales@travis-and-emery.com .

© Travis & Emery 2010

www.ingramcontent.com/pod-product-compliance
Lightning Source LLC
Chambersburg PA
CBHW071702160426
43195CB00012B/1551